Javascript tips

Previous published books by the author:

ESP32 Simplified
Raspberry Pi Pico Simplified
Raspberry Pi Pico W Simplified

In Dutch

ESP32 Uitgelegd
Javascript tips

Javascript tips

Luc Volders

Javascript tips
English version

Copyright © 2023 by Luc Volders

First Printing: 2023

ISBN 978-1-4476-7373-6

http://lucstechblog.blogspot.com/

Contents

HTML...259

Introduction

This book is not a programming course for JavaScript. It is not even
an introduction to programming with this language. It is a book
containing solutions. How did that go again? How can I sort an array
by the length of its elements? Or how do I measure how long a
function takes to run? How do I give all my strings the same length?
How do I calculate the number of days between two dates? Just a few
of the questions you come across when programming.

This book provides answers to many of those questions. More than
500 short tips that quickly solve small problems

Each tip shows an example program. Often, there is a brief
explanation given that shows how the solution works. Outputs are
displayed through an alert on the screen or in the console. Sometimes
there are multiple solutions for the same problem. This book shows
them, so you have the option to choose the one that fits your
programming style best.

If you want an easy way to test the tips, you can use JSFiddle:
https://jsfiddle.net/.

Not only beginners but also advanced JavaScript developers will
discover new things in this book.

About the Author

Luc started programming when he was 17 years old and bought an RCA 1802 microcomputer system. Actually it wasn't more than a bag of chips with a keyboard and a display that looked like an old calculator. The system had to be programmed in machine code, hexadecimal code, which is lower level than assembler. At that time there was no internet yet and documentation was scarce, so he had to figure everything out himself.

A year later, he bought a PET (the predecessor of the Commodore 64), and then began writing technical articles for a magazine. With the arrival of the Commodore 64, Luc wrote some heavyweights for this, now as simple looked upon, machine. He created a complete database system and a fully functional accounting software that were both highly successful commercially.

Additionally, he coauthored a book about the CBM64 with Jan van Die, and regularly contributed to Dutch magazines such as Commodore Dossier and PCM.

Later, Luc wrote monthly for the Dutch Atari-ST magazine Start, followed by stories for the Dutch magazines Amiga Magazine and MacFan .

A few years went by where Luc lost all interest in computers. Then a friend introduced him to the just invented 3D printers. Luc got interested in the open source world. He built his own 3D printer, learned the Arduino language, and became hooked again.

The last few years, Luc has written several books about the Internet of Things specifically focusing on the ESP32 and Raspberry Pi Pico microcontrollers.

While working with IoT applications, JavaScript soon came into view, and that led to this book.

Luc maintains his own web log that has been visited more than 150 thousand times. Due to his original ideas, it was mentioned several times on prominent tech websites like Hackaday. You can find his blog here: **http://lucstechblog.blogspot.com**

Conventions

Javascript programmers tend to follow certain conventions. The Oxford Dictionary defines a convention as: a way in which something is usually done.

In this book, we follow some of our own conventions.

No CamelCase.
All variables are written in lower case. CamelCase is annoying and more prone to typing errors.
As this is a convention, feel free to use cAMELcASE to substitute the variable and function names in this book whenever you want.

var instead of let and const
There is nothing wrong with using var. People have used **var** instead of **let** and **const** for eons. Make sure you define all your variables at the beginning of your program and document everything. **Let** and **Const** are for lazy programmers.
However there are no laws, just conventions so you can substitute var with let and const whenever you, or your company, want.

The use of Brackets
Often Javascript functions and if statements are written like this:

```
Function test(){
if (test == test){
alert("test")
}}
```

In this book, things are done differently. We write the function as follows:

```
Function test()
  {
    if (test == test)
      {
       alert("test")
      }
  }
```

You might like it, or you might not. However, the author and editors find this way of structuring functions and comparisons much clearer.
Again, there are conventions and there is free will.

HTML code

In this book, HTML code is used to build webpages.
A webpage generally starts and ends like this:

```
<!DOCTYPE html>
<html>
<head>
<title>Javascript tips</title>
</head>
<body>

<h1>A test for a tip</h1>

<button type="button" onclick="function test">Click
me</button>

<script>
var test = 1;
var test2 = 2;
function test()
  {
   alert(test1 + test2)
  {
</script>

</body>
</html>
```

As we presume that you have some basic knowledge about building websites, we only show the significant parts like this:

HTML part:

```
<h1>A test for a tip</h1>

<button type="button" onclick="function test">Click
me</button>
```

Javascript part:

```
<script>
var test = 1;
var test2 = 2;
function test()
  {
   alert(test1 + test2)
  {
</script>
```

Vanilla Javascript
All snippets and examples in this book are written in plain vanilla
Javascript. We do not cover frameworks like Angular, Jquery, React, Vue,
etc. etc. Although most of the snippets and examples can be used inside
these frameworks we have not tested this, so no guarantees.

The chapters
We have tried to arrange the tips and snippets in a logical way. The book is
divided in chapters, and each chapter shows tips and snippets for that
particular subject.

Let's start and have fun.

Numbers

0 before a number changes it to base 8

If you accidentally type a 0 in front of a number, the base will change to 8. Let us look at an example.

```
var number = 011;
alert(number);
```

Alert will show the number 9. This is because 011 in base 8 is $(0 * 0) + (1 * 8) + (1) = 9$.

Add True to a number

True and false are Boolean variables. However, true also has the value 1, and false the value 0.

```
var a = 5;
var b = true;

alert(a + b) will give 6.
```

We can use this as an example to test how often the outcome of a function is true. Here is an example where we count how many times the letter o appears in a text. Every time (a.charAt(i)=="o") is true, the value of counto is incremented.

```
var text = "The author of this book is Luc Volders"
var counto=0;
var i;

for (i=0; i<a.length; i++)
{
counto = counto + (a.charAt(i)=="o");
}
alert(counto);
```

Convert binary to a decimal integer

Use the next snippet to convert a binary number in a string to an integer.

```
test = "11111111"
alert(parseInt(test, 2));
```

Convert an integer to a float

If you need to convert an integer to a floating point value, you can use the commands:

```
var int = 25;
var float = parseFloat(int).toFixed(2);
console.log(float);
```

The number in toFixed(2) decides how many figures are added behind the decimal point.

Convert a number to binary

Here is a quick way to convert a number to its binary value. The outcome is a string.

```
var a = (14 >>> 0).toString(2)
alert(a + " " + typeof a);
```

Convert a number into an integer

Using Math.floor() , Math.ceil() or Math.round() we can convert a floating point number to an integer. However, the outcome is different for positive and negative numbers. If you just want to truncate the number, you can use the following code.

```
alert(23.9 | 0);
alert.log(-23.9 | 0);
```

The alerts will first show 23 and then -23

If you use this code on a string the outcome will be 0.

Convert a number into a string

Here is an easy way to convert a number (integer or float) to a string:

```
var value = 33.15 + "";

alert(value);
alert(typeof value);
```

By adding an empty string to a number, the number will be converted to a string.

Convert a number into a string 2

Using string literals, we can easily add variables to a string like this:

```
var amount = 10;
alert(`Hi the amount to pay is ${amount}`);
```

We can also use string literals to convert numbers to strings in this way:

```
var stringnumber = `${amount}`;
alert(typeof stringnumber);
```

Count the amount of digits in a number

We humans can see in a wink that 9000 is a number in the thousands
because it has 4 digits. If you want to check that in Javascript use the next
code.

```
var number = 2353454;
var a = number.toString();
alert(a.length)
```

This way, you can determine if a number is in tens, hundreds, or thousands,
etc.

Create even numbers

To create even numbers, you start with 0 or 2 (or any other even number)
and keep adding 2.

```
var even = 2;

for (i = even; i<11; i=i+2)
  {
   console.log (i)
  }
```

Create odd numbers

To create odd numbers, start with 1 (or any other odd number) and keep adding 2.

```
var odd = 1;

for (i = odd; i<11; i=i+2)
  {
   console.log (i)
  }
```

Get a number out of a string

If you need to get a number out of a string that contains both text and a number, you can use regex to achieve this.

```
var string = "€25.00 Euro";
var number = string.replace(/[^0-9.]/g, "");

alert(number);
```

The alert will show 25.00

Get all prime numbers up to a certain value

Prime numbers are often used in math calculations and in cryptography. The next snippet shows an easy way to get all prime numbers up until a certain value, which is 100 in this example.

```
for (var prime = 1; prime <= 100; prime++)
    {
    var a = false;
    for (var i = 2; i <= prime; i++)
        {
```

```
if (prime%i===0 && i!==prime)
    {
    a = true;
    }
}
if (a === false)
    {
    document.write(prime +"<br>");
    }
}
```

The test to see if a number is a prime-number is done by: if (prime%i===0
&& i!==prime)
A number is only a prime number when it is divisible by 1 and itself. If a
number divided by another number has a remainder of 0 (modulus 0), then
it is only divisible by itself.

How many figures behind the decimal point

If you want to know how many figures there are behind the decimal point,
you can use the following code.

```
var amount = 3.142857142857;
var count;

    var teststring = String(amount);
    if (teststring.includes('.'))
    {
        count = teststring.split('.')[1].length;
    }
    else
    {
    count = 0;
    }

alert(count)
```

The alert will show that there are 12 figures behind the decimal point.
If you entered an integer, then the variable count will have 0 as its value.

Random number from 1 to N

To obtain a random number between 1 and N, use the next snippet.

```
var number = Math.floor(Math.random() * N + 1);
```

You need to add 1 to Math.floor(Math.random() * N) because the outcome of this formula might be 0.

Random number within a range

Using Math.random() you can generate a random number between 0 and 1. To generate a random number between a minimum and maximum, you will need to multiply the Math.random() value with the difference between the minimum value and maximum value +1. The +1 is needed as otherwise the maximum number is not included. Here is an example snippet that shows how to do this.

```
var min = 5;
var max = 15;
function randomminmax(min, max)
{
    var random = Math.random() * (max - min + 1);
    var whole = Math.floor(random) + min;
    return whole;
}

document.write(randomminmax(min,max));
```

Random number with 5 digits

To generate a random number with 5 digits you can use the following code:

```
var val = Math.floor(1000 + Math.random() * 9000);
```

Remove the last x figures from a number

By making clever use of the OR function, we can remove any number of figures from the end of a number. Here is an example that demonstrates this.

```
alert(1234 / 10   | 0) // the result is 123
alert(1234 / 100  | 0) // the result is 12
alert(1234 / 1000 | 0) // the result = 1
```

Remove the leading 0

Removing a leading 0 in a number inside a string can be done like this:

```
var number = String(parseInt("0250"));
alert (number);
```

The command parseInt() removes the first zeros and the rest of the text. The string number will afterwards only contain "250"

Reverse a number

If you need to reverse a number you can use the following code.

```
number = number +"";
number = number.split("");
number = number.reverse();
number = number.join("");
number = +number;

alert(typeof number);
```

You can combine these commands into one line:

```
number =+((number+"").split("").reverse().join(""))
```

Round a number so it is divisible by x

The next snippet shows how to round a number up so it can be divided by
another number, and the outcome is an integer.

Math.ceil(x/y)*y;

Here, X is the number that needs to get divided, and y is the divider.

As an example yields Math.ceil(1021/3)*3 as outcome 1023. This is
because 341 x 3 = 1023.

Using Math.floor(x/y)*y rounds the number down. In our example the
outcome therefore will be 1020.

Round a number to 0.05

The following snippet shows how to round a figure to the nearest 5 cents.

```
alert (Math.round(amount * 20) / 20);
```

If amount has the value of 6.82 alert will show 6.8. If amount is 6.84 alert
shows 6.85

Round a number to 0.10

If you need to round amounts to 10 cents, you can do that easily with this
snippet.

```
alert (Math.round(amount * 10) / 10);
```

If amount has the value of 6.87 alert will show 6.9.

Round a number to 0.20

Rounding a number to 20 cents is easy with the following snippet.

```
alert (Math.round(amount * 5) / 5);
```

If amount is 6.3 the alert will show 6.4

Round a number to 0.25

Rounding a number to .25 is easy with the following snippet.

```
alert (Math.round(amount * 4) / 4);
```

If amount has the value of 6.3 then the alert will show 6.25

Round a number to 0.50

Rounding amounts to 50 cents can be done with the following snippet:

```
alert (Math.round(amount * 2) / 2);
```

If amount has the value 6.74 alert will show 6.5. If amount is 6.75 alert shows 7.

Rounding to a fixed number decimals

Numbers are often floating points, which means that they have a lot of decimal places. We can easily round numbers to a fixed amount of decimal places.

```
var testnum =6.58436;
testnum = testnum.toFixed(4);
```

The variable testnum will now be 6.5844. toFixed(4) rounds it to 4 decimal places.

Rounding with toFixed changes a number into a string

We can round a number to a fixed number of decimals with the following line:

```
number = number.toFixed(2);
```

Be aware that the command toFixed() changes the number into a string.

For example:

```
var testnum = 6.58436;
testnum = testnum.toFixed(2);
alert(testnum)
alert(typeof(testnum));
```

The alert box will display: 6.58 and then "string"

Split a number in its decimal part and fraction

Splitting a number in the part before and after the comma is easy.

```
var number = 3.142857142857;
var teststring = String(number);

var beforecomma = teststring.split('.')[0];
var behindcomma = teststring.split('.')[1];
```

Split a number in its figures

If you need to split a number into its figures it is best to first convert it into a string and then use split to put the figures in array elements. Here is an example.

```
var number = 123;
var string = number.toString();
var figures = string.split("");
alert (figures)
```

This can be combined into one statement:

```
figures = number.toString().split("");
```

Split a number into thousands, hundreds, etc.

If there is a number that we need to split into thousands, hundreds, tens etc we can do that with the following code:

```
var amount = 518234;
var helperarray = (amount+"").split("");
var amountlength = helperarray.length;
var units =[];
for (i=0; i<amountlength; i++)
{
units.push(helperarray[i]*Math.pow(10,amountlength-
(i+1)));
}
```

```
document.write(units);
```

As the amount is 518234 the alert will show 500000,10000,8000,200,30,4

Test if a number is an integer

Here is a quick way to test whether a number is an integer.

```
alert (23.5 % 1 === 0);
```

The alert will show "false" as the figure divided by 1 has a remainder of 0.5 which is not equal to zero.

Test if a number is an integer 2

Testing whether a number is an integer can be done with the following code.

```
var testnumber = "10.5";
if (testnumber === parseInt(testnumber, 10))
{
    alert("Integer!")
}
else
{
    alert("Not an integer!")
}
```

Another method is by using Math.floor:

```
if (testnumber == Math.floor(testnumber))
```

Both methods work with numbers and strings that contain a number. However, if the string, for example is "10C" is then Math.floor() gives Nan and the snippet shows "Not an integer"

Test if a number is an integer 3

Testing if a number is an integer can be done with regex. Here is an example.

```
var number = 12345
var isnumber = /^\d+$/.test(number);
if (isnumber)
{
  alert("The number is an integer")
}
```

Test if a number is positive or negative

A quick way to determine if a number is positive or negative is to use Math.sign(number) Math.sign() returns 1 for a positive number and -1 for a negative number.

Here are some examples.

```
alert(Math.sign(5));
alert(Math.sign(-5));
alert(Math.sign(0));
```

Test whether the input is a number

During a calculation, an error will be generated when one of the variables is not a number. This will stop your program. We can easily overcome this, as the next snippet shows.

```
var testnum = Number(prompt("Pick a number"));

if (!isNaN(testnum))
  {
  alert("The solution  =  " + testnum * 3);
```

```
     }
else
  {
  alert("Your input is not a number");
  }
```

The program will ask for a number. If you enter a number, an alert will show the number x 3. If you enter a word or random letters, the program will generate an alert but it will not stop.

Using !isNaN() we can test whether the variable is indeed a number.

Test if a variable is a number

To test whether a variable is a number or a string, we can use the command typeof. Unfortunately, this is not always reliable.

```
alert(typeof +"a10.1");
```

The alert shows that it is a number while a10.1 is not.

The accurate way to test whether a string is a number is as follows.

```
var  value = +"a10.1";
if (Number.isNaN(+value))
{
   alert ("Not a number");
}
else
{
   alert ("Yes it is a number")
}
```

Test if a variable is a number 2

Here is a fast way to test whether a variable is a number or a string.

```
var test = Number("Luc");
alert (test);
```

The variable test will give Nan (not a number) in the alert

Test for even or odd

Sometimes you need to test whether a number is even or odd. This can easily be done with the modulus function. When a number is divided by 2 and the remainder is 0 the number is even.

```
function iseven(number)
{
        if (number%2 == 0)
                return "even";
        else
                return "odd";
}
```

Call this function as follows:

```
alert(iseven(9));
```

Test for prime number

Prime numbers are used in computer science to encrypt data or passwords. It is beyond the scope of this book to explain how that is done, but you can find examples on the Internet. The next bit of code tests whether a number is a prime number or not and gives true or false as the result.

```javascript
function testifprime(value)
{
  if (value===1)
  {
    return false;
  }
  if(value === 2)
  {
    return true;
  }
  if (value > 2)
  {
    for(var x = 2; x < value; x++)
    {
      if(value % x === 0)
      {
        return false;
      }
    }
    return true;
  }
}

alert(testifprime(4));
alert(testifprime(155035219));
```

Underscore in a number

A peculiarity of Javascript is that it accepts an underscore as part of a number. Just try the next snippet.

```javascript
var number = 1_000;
alert(5_5 * number);
```

The alert will give the right answer being 55000.

Here is another example.

```
var number = 1_0_0_0;
alert(5_5 * number);
```

This only works with integers.

Use = as part of a calculation

Normally, we use = to get a result. We can, however, also use = as part of a calculation.

```
var number1 = 100;
var number2 = 200;

var number2 = 300 - (number1 = number2/number1);

alert( number1 );
alert( number2 );
```

The calculation first assigns number2/number1 to variable number1, which then will be 2. Then number2 gets the value 300 - number1. So the alerts will show first 2 and then 298.

Using switch-case with comparisons

It is not possible to use switch-case statements with comparisons like < or > in a standard way. However, there are ways to achieve that. The next snippet shows how you can do it.

```
function maxspeed(kmperhour)
    {
     var okspeed = "";
     switch (true)
       {
       case isNaN(kmperhour):
       okspeed = "Wrong input";
```

```
            break;

        case (kmperhour > 100):
        okspeed = "too speedy";
        break;
            case (kmperhour <= 100):
                okspeed = "doing ok";
                break;

            default:
                okspeed = "hmmmm";
                break;
            };
      return okspeed;
      }
alert(maxspeed(90));
```

Use + to convert a string into a number

Adding the values of two strings can not be done with the + sign.

```
var a = "5";
var b = "2";
```

a + b will then be "52" the strings will be concatenated instead of added.

The function Number() which converts strings to numbers (watch the capital N):
Number(a) + Number(b) will give 7 as an answer just like we want.

You can also achieve this with the + sign. If you put a + in front of a string that string will be converted to a number:

+a + +b will give 7 as an answer.

Other calculations like * and / will automatically convert strings to numbers.

Notes about numbers

Strings

Add a word or character at a certain position in a string

If you need to insert a word or character at a certain position in a string, you can use the following snippet

```
var a = "I want Javascript tips";
var b = " the book";
var position = 6;
var output = [a.slice(0, position), b,
a.slice(position)].join('');
alert(output);
```

The string is spliced at the sixth character, then the extra words are added, and then the rest of the string is added. Alert will show: "I want the book Javascript tips"

Build a string with n letters

If you need to build a string that contains n letters, you can use the next code:

```
var str = new Array(len + 1).join( character );
```

Here is an example that builds a string of 10 times the letter z

```
var str = new Array(10 + 1).join( "z" );
alert(str)
```

Build a string with n words

If you need to build a string that contains the same word n times, you can use the next code.

```
var str = new Array(len + 1).join( word );
```

Here is an example that builds a string with 10 times the word Javascript

```
var str = new Array(10 + 1).join( "Javascript " );
alert(str)
```

Change the first letter of every word in uppercase

This snippet shows how to change the first letter of each word in a string into uppercase. This can be done by splitting the words into an array, then change the first letter of each array element, and then converting the array back into a string.

```
var phrase = "Javascript tips by luc volders";
var phrasearray = phrase.split(" ");
var length = phrasearray.length
for (i=0; i<length; i++)
{   phrasearray[i]=phrasearray[i].charAt(0).toUpperC
ase() + phrasearray[i].slice(1);
}
phrase = phrasearray.join(" ");
alert(phrase);
```

Change the first letter in a string to uppercase

To change the first letter of a string into uppercase we use charAt(0) and change it with toUpperCase(). Next the rest of the string is added with slice()

```
var sentence = "javascript tips";
sentence = sentence.charAt(0).toUpperCase() +
sentence.slice(1);
alert(sentence)
```

Convert an array to a string

It is very easy to make a string from an array.

```
var array = [1, 2, 3];
var teststring = array.toString();
```

teststring now contains: "1, 2, 3"

Convert a name into initials

To convert a full name to its initials, we first split the name into its first name and surname, and then we take the first letter of the first name and convert it to uppercase and add it to a new variable. Then we do the same with the last name.

```
var name = "Luc volders"
var namesplit = naam.split(" ");

var initials = namesplit[0].charAt(0).toUpperCase()
initials += namesplit[1].charAt(0).toUpperCase()
alert(initials)
```


Convert a string into an array

There are four ways to convert a string into an array, where each element is a letter from that string.

```
const string = 'Javascript tips';

var usingSplit = string.split('');
var usingSpread = [...string];
var usingArrayFrom = Array.from(string);
var usingObjectAssign = Object.assign([], string);
```

Fixed length strings

There are two commands that are not very well known, called padStart and padEnd, that can make life much easier. Using these commands, you can easily format columns on your screen by giving strings equal lengths.

Using padStart, you can add a number of letters or other characters to the beginning of your string and give the string a fixed length.

```
var temp = String(22.5);
var temp = temp.padStart(10, ".")
alert (temp);
```

The alert will now show 22.5

You can exchange the "." by any other character or number of characters. The length of 10 will not be exceeded.

```
var temp = String(5);
var temp = temp.padStart(10,"_");
alert(temp);
```

Alert will now show '_____5'

If you omit the character(s) the string will be filled with spaces.

padEnd does the same but adds to the end of the string.

```
var temp = String(5);
var temp = temp.padEnd(10,"*");
alert(temp);
```

The alert will show '5*********'

Generate a random password

Here is a quick and dirty way to generate a random password.

```
var password = "pw " +
Math.random().toString(16).slice(2)
alert(password)
```

Getting all figures in a text

The next program extracts all figures from a text. When you are building, for example, an IOT project, you often only need the figures, which can be sensor values.

```
var test = "temperature is 25 degrees"
var testnew = ""

for (let i=0; i<test.length; i++)
{
    if (+(test[i]))
        {
            testnew = testnew + test[i];
        }
}
alert(testnew)
```

The value that testnew shows in the alert is 25.

Get an amount or number out of a text

If you need to extract an amount or a number out of a string, you can use regex for that.

```
string.replace(/[^0-9\./]/g, '')
```

This extracts the decimals and the . from a string. Here is an example.

```
string = "the amount is 15,22"
alert(string.replace(/[^0-9\,/]/g, ''))
```

This only works if there is only one amount or number in the text.

Get the first word of a string

To get the first word of a string you can use:

```
var string = "Javascript is the language"
var firstword = string.split(" ")[0]

alert(firstword)
```

Get the last word of a string

To get the last word in a string, use the following snippet.

```
var month = "jan 30";
var temperature =
month.substring(month.lastIndexOf(" "));

alert(temperature);
```

You can also use the snippet discussed in the trick, where we split the first name and surname.

Get the last word of a string 2

Here is another way to get the last word in a string.

```
var a = "This is a test with Javascript"
alert(a.split(" ").pop())
```

Get the last x letters of a string

To get the last x letters of a string, you can use the next snippet:

```
var string = "123456789"
var result=string.slice(-4)
alert(result)
```

The command slice(-4) extracts the last 4 letters of the string.

If you need the third and fourth letters from the back you can change this in:

```
var string = "123456789"
var result=string.slice(-4, -2)
alert(result)
```

This takes the fourth letter from the back to the third letter. This results in figures 6 and 7. Using (-4, -1) would result in "678".

How many times does a character occur in a string

To count how many times a certain character occurs in a string, you can use the next snippet.

```
var string1 = "Javascript tips";
var letter = "s";
var total;
for (var i = total = 0; i < string1.length; total
+= (string1[i++] == letter));
alert(total);
```

This only works with single characters. If you want to test for characters and words, use the tip described in: How many times does a string occur in another string

How many times does a character occur in a string 2

Here are two methods to count how many times a letter occurs in a string. Both methods count how many times the letter i appears. Here is the first method.

```
var teststring = "Javascript tips";
var number = teststring.split("i").length-1
alert(number);
```

And here is the second method.

```
var teststring = "Javascript tips";
var number = (teststring.match(/i/g) || []).length
alert(number);
```

How many times do all characters or figures occur in a string

The next snippet builds an object that presents a list of the number of times each character or figure occurs in a string.

```
var string = 'aabb3333bc1dd55d';
var mapString = string => {
    const map = {};
    for(let i = 0; i < string.length; i++){
        map[string[i]] = (map[string[i]] || 0) + 1;
    };
    return map;
};
console.log(mapString(string));
```

How many times does a string occur in another string

Working with sensor readings, we sometimes want to know how often a certain reading occurs. In the next example, temperatures have been stored into a string. If we want to know how often a certain temperature occurs, we can use the following script lines:

```
var temp = "33.3 35.2 20.36 33.3 26.4 28.5 33.3";
var search = "33.3";

var regex = new RegExp(search, "gi");
var quantity = (temp.match(regex) || []).length;

alert(quantity);
```

How to check if a string only contains all the same characters

To test if a string contains all the same characters or a certain character, you can check the length of that string, remove the character, and test the length again. Here is an example.

```
var str = "     ";
var before = str.length
var str2=str.replaceAll(" ","")
after = str2.length
alert(before>after)
```

Insert a variable into a string

To insert a variable into a string we normally use the following method.

```
var age = "36"
var string = "I am now " + age + " year old"
alert(string)
```

Javascript now has a function called string literals ,which does the same. You can use it as follows.

```
var age = "36";
var string = `I am now ${age} year old`;
alert(string)
```

To use this you need to use back-ticks in the string definition.

Loop over a string

Here is a quick method to loop over a string:

```
var text = 'Javascript';

for (var value of text)
{
   console.log(value);
}
```

Make the first character after a colon a capital

When we make a string from an object, the result is text that includes a colon. For example, Name: luc Volders. To make sure that the first letter after the colon is capitalized, we can use the next function:

```
var data='name: luc Volders';
function capitalisefirst(name)
{
    return name.replace(/([:\?]\s+)(.)/g,
function(namecap)
      {
       return namecap.toUpperCase();
      });
}
```

61

```
alert(capitalisefirst(data));
```

The regular expression captures the first letter after the colon and toUpperCase() converts that to a capitalized letter.

new String creates an object

Please beware that if you use new String to copy or create a string, the result is not a string but an object. Here is an example.

```
var original = "A normal string";
var newstring = new String(original);
alert(typeof(newstring))
```

Quotes in a string

Sometimes we need to put a quote in a string. As quotation marks within quotation marks are not directly allowed, we need to use backslash to achieve what we want:

```
var string1 = "He said \"Hey this works\"";
```

Remove all numeric characters except the dot

The next line shows how to remove all non-numeric characters from a string except the figures and the decimal dot.

```
var string = "The temperature is 28.5 degrees C"
var temp = string.replace(/[^\d.-]/g, '');
alert(temp)
```

Please note that this only works if there is one number in the string.

Remove everything after a word or character

If you need to remove everything after a certain word or character in a string, you can use the next snippet.

```
var test = "Javascript tips, Luc Volders";
remaining = test.substring(0,
test.lastIndexOf(","));
alert (remaining)
```

In this example everything behind the comma is removed.

Remove everything except the characters from a string

The next snippet shows how to remove all characters from a string, except the letters.

```
var badstring = "12KLj mhg56"

var okstring = badstring.replace(/[^a-z]/gi, '')

alert(okstring)
```

Only the characters are shown. If you need the spaces to make full sentences add space to the regex expression like this:

```
okstring = badstring.replace(/[^a-z\s]/gi, '')
```

Remove the first and last characters from a string

The next code shows how to remove the first and last letter from a string.

```
var string = "*Javascript tips*";
var result = string.substring(1, string.length-1);
```

```
console.log(result);
```

Remove the first x characters from a string

To remove the first x letters of a string you can use the next snippet.

```
var amount = 6;
var teststring  = "Luc's Javascript tips";
var newstring = teststring.substring(amount,
teststring.length - amount);
alert(newstring);
```

Remove non alphabetic characters

The next program will filter all non-alphabetic characters (except space) from a string. What is left is pure text.

```
var test = "h3ell55o LUC"
var testnew = ""

for (let i=0; i<test.length; i++)
{
    if ((test[i].toLowerCase() !==
test[i].toUpperCase()) || test[i] == " ")
        {
            testnew = testnew + test[i];
        }
}
```

```
alert(testnew)
```

The for loop tests each character to see if it is, when converted to lowercase, equal to uppercase. If that is true, it is rejected. If this is not true, the character is added to the new string. In this example the text hello LUC will be shown in the alert.

Remove numbers from a string

To remove any numbers from a string you can use the following code.

```
var mixedtext = "Javascript 456 tips";

text = mixedtext.replace(/[0-9]/g, '');

alert(text);
```

Remove spaces in front and behind a string

When you want to remove spaces in front and behind a string, you can use the built-in trim() function. Unfortunately that function does not work in all browsers. To get the same functionality you can use the following.

```
var teststring = "        Javascript tips        ";

alert(teststring + " : " + teststring.length)

var test2 = teststring.replace(/^\s+|\s+$/gm,'');
alert(test2 + " : " + test2.length)
```

The first alert will show the length as 27, The second alert will show the trimmed length as 15

Remove the first n words of a string

To remove the first n words from a string, use the following example.

```
var teststring  = "A rather long sentence from
Javascript tips";
var remove = 5;
```

```
teststring = teststring.split("
").slice(remove).join(' ');

alert(teststring);
```

Remove the last word from a string

To remove the last word from a string, use the next snippet.

```
var teststring= "Remove the last word";

teststring = teststring.substring(0,
teststring.lastIndexOf(" "));
```

Remove the last x characters from a string

To remove the last x letters from a string, you can use the next snippet.

```
var amount = 5;
var teststring  = "Luc's Javascript tips";
var newstring = teststring.substring(0,
teststring.length - amount);
alert(newstring);
```

Replace part of a string case insensitive

One of the previous tips showed how to change part of a string into something else. That only functioned case-dependently. The next snippet shows how to replace a part of a text case-insensitive.

The regex expression gi is used to search global and case insensitive.

```
var teststring = "Javascript javascript"
```

```
var result = teststring.replace(/j/gi, "J");
alert (result)
```

Replace all occurences in a string

To replace certain characters in a string. we can use String.replace().
However, that will only replace the first occurrence in a string. If we want
to replace all occurrences, you can use regex like shown here.

```
var teststring = "luc luc";
alert(teststring.replace("l", "L"));
```

This is the normal method, and alert will show "Luc luc" which is not what
we want.

```
var teststring = "luc luc";
alert(teststring.replace(/l/g, "L"));
```

Now the alert shows "Luc Luc" which is what we were trying to achieve.
Just be careful, as this will replace all occurrences of "l" in "L". If you do
not want that to happen, search for a more specific string, as the next
example shows.

```
var teststring = "luc letters level luc";
alert(teststring.replace(/lu/g, "Lu"));
```

Replace the first letter of the first word with a capital

Not everyone enters text neatly. Sometimes people omit capitals as the first
letter of a sentence. The next program corrects this.

```
var origtext = "hello. this is a test. the last
line."
var helptxt = "";
var helpar = origtext.split(". ");
```

```
for (number in helpar)
{
helptxt = helpar[number][0].toUpperCase();
helptxt = helptxt +
helpar[number].slice(1,helpar[number].length);
helpar[number] = helptxt;
}

origtext = helpar.join(". ");
alert(origtext);
```

First, the text is split into separate lines in an array. Then the first character of each array entry is converted to uppercase. Then the rest of the sentence is added, and the corrected text is stored back into the array. Lastly, the array is converted to the original single variable, in which we replace the array's comma separator with ". "

Replace spaces in underscore and characters in uppercase

The next example is only meant as an example of replacing multiple items in one command. We are going to replace all spaces in a string into _ (underscore) and at the same time convert all letters to uppercase.

```
var testline = "This is a test. Two lines";
var converted = testline.replace(/
/g,'_').toUpperCase();
console.log(converted);
```

Replace without regex

If you want to replace certain characters or words in a string but are not fluent in regex: no worries. Here is another method.

```
var teststring = "luc letters level luc";
```

```
teststring = teststring.replaceAll('lu','Lu')
alert(teststring)
```

ReplaceAll will replace all occurrences of "lu" into "Lu"

Another option would be to use split() to split the string at the letters "lu" and then join them again with "Lu" like this:

```
string = string.split('lu').join('Lu')
```

You could even do this in a while loop:

```
var teststring = "luc letters level luc";
while (teststring.includes('lu'))
    teststring = teststring.replace('lu', 'Lu')
alert(teststring)
```

Reverse the characters in a string

Javascript has a built-in function for reversing the elements in an array. There is no such function for reversing the characters in a string. Here is a function that achieves this.

```
var teststring;
var newstring;

function turnaround(teststring)
{
    if((typeof teststring) !== "string")
      {
      return;
      }
    var numberletters = teststring.length;
    newstring='';
    while(numberletters > 0)
      {
      numberletters --;
      newstring += teststring[numberletters];
```

```
        }
    return newstring;
}

alert("The reversed string is: " + turnaround("spiT
tpircsavaJ"));
```

Reverse the characters in a string 2

To reverse the characters in a string, we can convert the string to an array,
reverse the array elements, and join them to a string. The next snippet does
that.

```
function turnaround(teststring)
{
return [...teststring].reverse().join('');
}

test = turnaround("spiT tpircsavaJ");
alert (test);
```

If you do not want to use the spread operator you can use split() instead:

```
return teststring.split("").reverse().join('');
```

Reverse the characters in a string 3

We can reverse the letters into a string by splitting the string in array
elements, then reversing the elements and joining them back into a string.
Here is an example.

```
function turnaround(string){
    return string.split("").reverse().join("");
}
turned = (turnaround("olleh"))
```

```
alert(turned)
```

Safely combine multiple variables into a string

If you need to combine several variables,which can be strings and numbers, into one use concat().

```
var first = 1;
var second = "2";
var third = 3;

var combined = "".concat(first, second, third);
```

This will make a string containing "123".

Search a string on the x'th occurence

Take a look at the next string.

```
var string = "Basic C++ Javascript Basic Lua Basic
Python Basic";
```

If you need to know at what position the 3d occurrence of Basic is, you can use the next snippet.

```
function where(string, subString, index)
{
   return string.split(subString,
index).join(subString).length;
}

console.log(where(string, 'Basic', 3))
```

Change the number 3 for the third occurrence into any other number you need. If you pass an out-of-range number, the length of the string will be displayed.

Shorten a string

If you need to show several words that all have the same length, you must shorten them to that length. You can do this with substr(0,x) where 0 is the starting character and x the last character.

```
var line =
"==================================================";
alert(line.substr(0,9);
```

This also makes it easy to create lines of different lengths without having to manually fill in the "=" each time.

Sort a strings characters

When needed, you can sort the letters in a string with the following line of code:

```
alert ("Javascript
tips".split("").sort().join(""));
```

Sort the words in a string on their length

To sort the words in a string according to their length, you can use the following snippet.

```
var text = 'Python Javascript C++';
function sortonlength()
```

```
  {
    var textarray = text.split(' ');
    var sorted = textarray.sort(function(a, b)
    {
        return a.length - b.length;
    })
    return sorted.join(' ');
};
alert(sortonlength(text));
```

By making a small adjustment, you can also use this to sort an array by the length of its elements.

Split first name and surname

To split a name into a first name and surname, you can use the next snippet.

```
var name = "Luc Volders";
var firstname;
var surname;
[firstname, surname] = name.split(" ");
alert(firstname);
alert(surname);
```

In this snippet, destructuring is used to split the name.

Split a text in multiple lines

For convenience you can split a string in multiple lines.

```
testext = "This is \
a text \
of multiple \
lines";
```

```
alert(testext);
document.write(testext);
```

The \ will not be part of the text.

Strange addition

Javascript has some strange features. Just try the next snippet.

```
alert(("b" + "a" + + "a" + "a").toLowerCase())
```

Subtraction of an integer from a string yields the result as a string.

We all know that if you use + to combine strings with numbers, the string is concatenated in-stead of the numbers being added.

```
"" + 10 + 5 + 21
```

This will build this string : "10521"

```
2023 + "5" will build this string : "2028"
```

However, subtracting yields a totally different result. Subtracting a number from a string will yield the answer as a string.

```
2023 - "8" will yield "2015" just like
```

```
"2023" - 8 will also yield "2015"
```

Test if a character is a letter or a sign

We can test individual characters in a string to see if they are a letter or a sign. The trick is to convert signs to capitals; they remain the same.

```
character = "!";
alert(character.toUpperCase() !==
character.toLowerCase())
```

Signs will have true as value, and so will figures. Their uppercase and lowercase are the same. Letters like a-z will change into A-Z and therefore will give false.

Test if a character or word is present in a string

Here is a quick test to check whether a character or word is present in a string.

```
var text = "this is a test"

if (text.indexOf("is") >-1)
   {
   console.log("the searched word is present")
   }
```

indexOf(0 points to the place where the searched word is in the string. So if it's value is 0 or larger, it is present. Beware that in the searched string must be an exact match. In this example "is" is two times found in "this" and "is".

Test if a character or word is present in a string 2

Using text.startsWith allows us to test whether a character or word is at the beginning of a string.

```
var string = "Hello world"
alert(string.startsWith("Hello")
```

The alert will display "true"

We can add a second parameter to have the search start further on in the string, like this:

```
var string = "Hello world"
search = string.startsWith("world",5)
alert (search)
```

This time the alert will display "false" as the word world is at the sixth position. Counting starts here at 0.

Test if a string is an anagram

The following code snippet demonstrates how to determine whether a string is an anagram of another string.

```
function testanagram(string1, string2)
{
string1test =
string1.toLowerCase().split('').sort().join('');
string2test =
string2.toLowerCase().split('').sort().join('');
return string1test == string2test;
}


alert(testanagram('listen', 'silent'));
alert(testanagram('loop', 'polo'));
alert(testanagram('this', 'shit'));
```

Test if a string is a palindrome

A palindrome is a word that backwards is the same word. Examples are civic, racecar and madam. The next lines show how to test if a word or sentence is a palindrome.

```
var string = "racecar";
var strReverse =
string.split("").reverse().join("");

if (string === strReverse) {
  alert("This is a palindrome");
} else {
  alert("No, this is not a palindrome");
}
```

Test if a string contains numbers

If you need to know whether there are numbers in a string, you can use the next snippet.

```
teststring = "Temperature is 23 degrees"
result =/\d/.test(teststring)
alert(result)
```

Test if a text is present in another text

If you need to know if a text occurs in another text, you can use the following snippet:

```
var string = "Hello"
var searchstring = "llo"
console.log(string.includes(searchstring))
```

Test whether two strings are case-insensitive equal

In a computer, you might get input from a user that exactly matches what you are looking for, but the user only uses lower case or a mix of upper and lower case, whereas your text is the same but the lower/upper case option is different. Here's how you can find out.

```
var text1 = 'An example';
var text2 = 'an Example';

text1 = text1.toLowerCase();
text2 = text2.toLowerCase();

equaltest = (text1 === text2);

console.log(equaltest);
```

The log will show true.

Use padStart to add predecessor characters

Using padStart we can add characters (numbers or strings) at the beginning of a string. We need to supply the number of characters and which characters to use. Here are a few examples to clarify.

```
var test = "6";
var test2 = "25";

alert (test.padstart(4,0));
alert (test2.padstart(2,0));
```

The first alert shows 0006 because we indicate that the result should become 4 characters and that the leading characters should be 0.
The second alert will show 25 because we indicated that the result should be a string of maximum of 2 characters, which it already is.

```
var minute = 3
alert (minute.toString().padStart(2,0));
```

In this example, the number 3 is converted to a string, and padStart puts a 0 in front of it.

```
var minute = 3
alert (minute.toString().padStart(20,"-*"));
```

We can put multiple characters behind the comma. In this example, the number 3 is converted to a string and multiple -* are put in front untill a total of 20 characters is reached.

Which letter corresponds with a number

Our alphabet consists of the letters a-z and we have the capital A-Z. So 26 letters and 26 capitals. If we have a number and want to know its corresponding letter, we can use the next code.

```
function letter(number)
{
    if(number < 1 || number > 26 || typeof number !
== 'number')
    {
        return -1;
    }
    var start = 96;
    return String.fromCharCode(number + start);
};
alert(letter(26));
```

The numbers from 1 to 26 correspond with the letters a-z. If you change var start = 96; to var start = 64; you will get the corresponding capitals.

Which place has a letter in the alphabet

This tip reverses the tip "Which letter corresponds with a number". We have a letter and want to know where its place in the alphabet is. We can find that as follows.

```
letter = "A"
const ascii = tekst.charCodeAt(0);
alert(ascii)
```

If the letter is a capital, the alert will give a value from 65 (A) to 90 (Z) otherwise, the value will be from 97 (a) to 122 (z).

Notes about strings

Date

Advance the time with x seconds

This example shows how you can advance the time with x seconds.

```
var now;
now = new Date('2023-01-01 23:59:55');
alert(now.getMinutes() + ':' + now.getSeconds());
now.setSeconds(now.getSeconds() + 10);
alert(now.getMinutes() + ':0' + now.getSeconds());
alert(now)
```

Using now.setSeconds() we add 10 seconds to the current time in this example. In this particular case, the time will change from 23 hour 59 minutes and 5 seconds to 5 seconds after midnight, and therefore the date will alter automatically.

Advance the time 30 minutes

If you want to set the time 30 minutes forward, you can do that with setMinutes() and getMinutes like the next snippet shows.

```
var testdate = new Date();
testdate.setMinutes( testdate.getMinutes() + 30 );
alert( testdate );
```

Use -30 to go 30 minutes back in time.

Advance the time one day

If you need tomorrow's date, you can do that by adding 1 to todays date.

```
var now = new Date();
var tomorrow = new Date();
tomorrow.setDate(now.getDate() + 1);
```

```
alert('Now:  ' + now);
alert('Tomorrow:  ' + tomorrow);
```

Change 24 hour notation to 12 hour

To change 24 hour clock notation to 12 hour notation, we just have to take the hours modulus 12.

```
var today = new Date();
var hour = today.getHours();
alert(hour);
alert(hour %12);
```

Comparing dates

To compare two dates we can not simply use == or ===

```
var d1 = new Date("09/22/2020");
var d2 = new Date("09/22/2020");
alert (d1 === d2);
```

The above alert will show "false". The right way to do this is:

```
alert (d1.toString() === d2.toString());
```

Comparing dates 2

Comparing dates may lead to a false outcome when the time is taken into account. The dates may be the same, but the time part may differ. Set the time to zero to compare the dates. The following example shows how to achieve this.

```
var date1, date2
date1 = new Date();
date1.setHours(0,0,0,0);
alert(date1);
date2 = new Date( "May 12, 2023" );
alert(date2);
if (date1.getTime() === date2.getTime())
  {
   alert("The dates are equal.");
  }
  else
  {
   alert("The dates differ.");
  }
```

Comparing dates 3

We wish to compare two variables that contain dates that are somewhere in our program.

```
var date1 = "09/12/2020";
var date2 = "08/05/2020";
```

To compare these dates, we have to transform them into Date Objects. This can be done using new Date().

```
date1 = new Date(date1);
date2 = new Date(date2);
```

Now we can easily compare these dates:

```
datum1 > datum2;   //true
datum2 < datum1;   //false
datum1 >= datum2; //true
datum1 <= datum2; //false
datum1 == datum2; // false
```

Convert a given time to seconds

If you have a variable that holds the time in Hour, minutes, and seconds and you need to know how many seconds this is, you can get that number as follows.

```
var time = "2:1:20";
var timearray = time.split(":");
alert("The time is = " + timearray);
var seconds = (+timearray[0]) * 60 * 60 +
(+timearray[1]) * 60 + (+timearray[2]);
alert("The total number of seconds  = "+seconds);
```

The time is put into a variable with the name time in the hh:mm:ss format. The time variable is split into an array, and each element is converted to the number of seconds.

Convert seconds to hours and minutes

The next function converts the number of seconds into hours and minutes.

```
var totsecs = 3722;
function secstohour()
{
    var hours = parseInt(totsecs / 3600);
    var minutes = parseInt((totsecs - (hours *
3600)) / 60);
    var time = hours + " hour and " + minutes + "
minutes"
    return time;
};
alert(secstohour(totsecs));
```

The total number of seconds (totsecs) is divided by 3600 (the number of seconds in an hour) and the rest is divided by 60 to get the number of minutes. Both figures are made into integers to avoid getting fractions.

Convert seconds to hours and minutes 2

The following code can be used to convert a large number of seconds into hours, minutes, and seconds. The next example shows how to convert 3600 seconds into minutes.

```
var date = new Date(0);
date.setSeconds(3600);
var time = date.toISOString().substr(11, 8);
console.log(time)
```

Convert the date to everyday speech

Using alert(new Date(2023,0,1)) we can get the date but it is presented like this: Sun Jan 01 2023 00:00:00 GMT+0100

The command toLocaleDateString allows us to transform this to everyday speech. To achieve this we need to set some options. Here is how to do that.

```
var options = { weekday: 'long', year: 'numeric',
month: 'long', day: 'numeric' };
var today  = new Date(2023,0,1);

today = today.toLocaleDateString("en-US", options);
alert(today)
```

The variable today is a string and the alert shows: "Sunday, January 1, 2023" which is more pleasant to read

Create a random date

The next snippet shows how to create a random date between a start date and today's date.

```javascript
function makedate(start, end) {
    return new Date(start.getTime() + Math.random()
* (end.getTime() - start.getTime()));
}

var createddate = makedate(new Date(2000,0,0), new
Date());
alert(createddate)
```

In this example, the start date is the year 2000, but you can replace it with any date of your choice. You can also change the second date to create a boundary like this:

```javascript
createddate = makedate(new Date(2000,0,0), new
Date(2001,0,0));
alert(createddate)
```

Every day of the week another function, value or picture

Use the next snippet to change the value of a variable, execute another function, show a different text or picture depending on the day of the week.

```javascript
var nowday=new Date().getDay()

if (nowday==1)
   {
     alert (1)
   }
else if (nowday==2)
    {
     alert(2)
```

```
    }
else if (nowday==3)
    {
     alert(3)
    }

...

else if (nowday==7)
    {
     alert(7)
    }
else

{
alert("wrong")
}
```

new Date().getDay() gives us the number of the day of the week. Days are numbered from 1 to 7. The if -else lines show therefore every day another alert which can be replaced by changing a value, another function, or replace a picture with another picture on your site.

Find the first and last day of the month

You can find the first and last day of a month using the next code.

```
var now = new Date();
var firstday = new Date(now.getFullYear(),
now.getMonth(), 1);
alert(firstday);
var lastday = new Date(now.getFullYear(),
now.getMonth() + 1, 0);
alert (lastday);
```

The first day of the month is found by setting the number of the day to 1. The last day is found by adding 1 to the number of the month and setting the number of the day to 0.

Get the user's time zone

If you are working with date and time related programs, it is important to get the user's timezone. Here is how to get the information.

```
zone =
Intl.DateTimeFormat().resolvedOptions().timeZone
alert(zone)
```

Give tomorrow's date or the date 20 days from now

Dates are often used in Javascript. Be it for keeping an agenda, keeping dates for customer orders, or lists with temperatures. Working with dates often requires to get a date in the future or in the past. The next function calculates a date by adding or subtracting a number of days.

```
function calcdate(from, amount)
{
   var newdate = new Date(from);
   newdate.setDate(newdate.getDate() + amount);
   return newdate;
}

var newdate = calcdate("09/20/2020",+150);
alert(newdate);
alert(newdate.getDate() + " " + (newdate.getMonth()
+1) + " " + newdate.getFullYear());
```

You need to use newdate.getMonth()+1 because the date index starts at 0

Give the name of the month

Using new.Date().getMonth() we can get the number of the month. If you need the name you will have to put the names in an array and use the number as the index. Here is an example.

```
var  months = ["January", "February", "March",
"April", "May", "June", "July", "August",
"September", "October", "November", "December"];

var today = new Date();
alert(today.getMonth());

var name = months[today.getMonth()];
alert(name)
```

Give yesterday's date or that of 20 days ago

We can use the tip "Give me the date of tomorrow or 20 days from now" the same way to test for yesterdays date or that of x days ago. The only thing you have to do is in the example:

```
var newdate = calcdate("05/12/2023",+150)
```

change into:

```
var newdate = calcdate("05/12/2023",-150)
```

Javascript automatically uses the lengths of the months and takes in account whether it is a leap year or not.

Give the date 4 months from now or 3 years from now

We will use the formula from the tip: Give me the date of tomorrow or 20 days from now

```
function calcdate(from, amount)
{
  var newdate = new Date(from);
  newdate.setDate(newdate.getDate() + amount);
  return newdate;
}
```

To calculate months in the future or past you need to change:

```
newdate.setDate(newdate.getDate() + amount);
```

into

```
newdate.setMonth(newdate.getMonth() + amount);
```

For calculating years you need to alter the formula in:

```
newdate.setFullYear(newdate.getFullyear() +
amount);
```

How many days between two dates

Suppose we have 2 dates. Todays date and August 31 2026. How many days are between those dates.

Start with defining two variables with the dates:

```
var date1 = new Date();
var date2 = new Date("08/31/2026");
```

Next step is to calculate the difference between the two dates:
```
var timedif = date2.getTime() - date1.getTime();
```

Last step is to transform this into days:

```
daysdif = Math.round(timedif / (1000 *3600 *24));
```

Math.round makes sure the number is rounded.
The formula 1000 (1 second) * 3600 (60 seconds * 60 minutes) *24 equals
1 day in seconds.

How many days in a specific month

To find the number of days in a specific month use the new Date function
while setting the number of days to 0. The next example explains this.

```
var numberdays = (new Date(2024, 2, 0).getDate());
alert(numberdays);
```

How many months between two dates

The following snippet shows how to calculate the number of months
between two dates.

```
function monthsbetween(date1, date2)
  {
     var d1 = date1, d2 = date2;
     if (date1 < date2)
        {
             d1 = date2;
             d2 = date1;
        }
     var month = (d1.getFullYear() -
d2.getFullYear()) * 12 + (d1.getMonth() -
d2.getMonth());
     if (d1.getDate() < d2.getDate())
     {
     --m;
```

```
        }
        return month;
    }

var date1 = new Date("12 May 2020");
var date2 = new Date("12 Jan 2021");
document.write("Months in between = " +
monthsbetween(date1,date2));
```

The test if (date1 < date2) and the following code make the function adjust automatically if date1 is more recent than date2 or the other way around. The calculation subtracts the two years, multiplies the outcome by 12, and adds the difference in months.

How many minutes between two dates

The next snippet calculates how many minutes there are between two dates.

```
function getmins(first, last)
{
    return (last - first) / (1000 * 60);
}

howlong = getmins(
    new Date('2021-08-17 09:00:00'),
    new Date('2021-08-17 10:00:00')
);

alert(howlong)
```

The calculation is done by subtracting the second date from the first and dividing that by (1000 * 60) as a minute is 60 seconds * 1000 milliseconds.

How many seconds between two dates

The next snippet calculates how many seconds there are between two dates.

```
function getsecs(first, last)
{
   return (last - first) / 1000;
}

howlong = getsecs(
   new Date('2021-08-17 09:00:00'),
   new Date('2021-08-17 18:00:00')
);

alert(howlong)
```

How many hours between two dates

The next snippet provides a function that calculates the number of hours between two dates.

```
function hours(first, last)
{
   alert((last - first) / (1000 * 60*60));
}

hours(
   new Date('2021-08-30'),
   new Date('2021-08-31')
);
```

How many years between two dates

To calculate the number of years between two dates first convert them both to milliseconds and then divide the number of milliseconds by the number of milliseconds in a year.

```
var datestring = "2023,02,01"
var dateinmillies = new Date() - new
Date(datestring);
var
years=Math.floor(dateinmillies/1000/60/60/24/365);
alert(years)
```

In what quarter do we live

The following snippet shows a function that you can use to determine which quarter a date is.

```
var newmonth = new Date().getMonth()+1
function findquarter()
{
    if (newmonth <= 3) {return 1}
      else if (newmonth <= 6) {return 2}
      else if (newmonth <= 9) {return 3}
      else if (newmonth <= 12) {return 4}
}

alert(findquarter(newmonth))
```

We start with finding the month with new Date().getMonth()+1 Mind that we have to add 1 to the month as months start with index 0 (january = month 0). Next an if-else test looks in which part of the year the month is.

In what quarter do we live 2

The next snippet shows a quick way to determine which quarter a date is in.

```
var newmonth = new Date().getMonth()+1
alert(Math.ceil(month/3)
```

In which century do we live

To know in what century we live, we have to divide the year by 100. If that is an integer (2000), then we have the century. If it is not an integer, we need to add 1.

```
function testcentury(year)
  {
  if (year/100 % 1 === 0)
    {
    return year/100;
    }
    else
    {
    return parseInt(year/100, 10)+1;
    }
  }
var century = testcentury(1885);
alert (century);
```

In which century do we live 2

Math.ceil() rounds numbers up to the nearest integer. We can use that to determine in an easy way in which century we live.

```
alert(Math.ceil(1999/100))
```

Is January first a Sunday ??

To know if January 1 in a certain year is a Sunday, you can use the next snippet.

```
var year = 2017;
var day = new Date(year, 0, 1);
if ( day.getDay() === 0 )
{
   document.write("January 1 in "+year+" is a
Sunday");
}
```

This can be used to examine any day of the year. The counting of the names of the days begins at 0 for Sundays. The counting of the months starts with 0 for January.

Is the given day a weekday or in the weekend

To know if a given day is a weekday or falls in the weekend we can use the getDay command. This gives the day in the week in numbers from 0 to 6, where 6 is Saturday, and 0 is Sunday.

The next program shows an alert that tells whether the chosen day is a weekday or in the weekend.

```
var date = new Date("2020-09-26");
var day = datum.getDay();

var weekend = (day === 6) || (day === 0);

if(weekend==true)
{
    alert("The chosen day is in a weekend");
} else
{
    alert("A weekday");
```

Is this year a leap year

To test whether a year is a leap year, we need to know if there is a February 29. Set the date to february 29, and if that day does not exists in the given year, the month will be set to March, which has index 2. So we test for index 1, which is February (Januari is 0).

```
function leap(year)
{
return new Date(year, 1, 29).getMonth() === 1;
}

alert(leap(2021));
alert(leap(2020));
```

Is this a leap year 2

There are several demands for a year to be a leap year. If it is a full century, then it should also be divisible by 100 AND 400. Next to that the year should be divisible by 4. So 1700 is not a leap year as it is divisible by 100 but not by 400. We can test this by a ternary operator.

```
function leapyear(year)
{
return (year % 100 === 0) ? (year % 400 === 0) :
(year % 4 === 0);
}

alert(leapyear(2100))
alert(leapyear(2200))
alert(leapyear(2020))
```

Make a copy of a date

If you need an exact copy of a date, you can use the next lines of code.

```
var now = new Date();
var nowcopy = new Date(now.getTime());
alert(nowcopy);
```

By using getTime() we get the exact time from the original date and copy that into the new variable. This makes sure that we have an exact copy of the date and time.

Measure how long an action takes

To get the time in milliseconds, you can use + new Date() If you put this at the start of a part of a program and at the end, you can measure how long it takes to complete the action. Here is an example that measures the time to calculate 1000.000 square roots.

```
var start = + new Date();
for (i=0; i<1000000; i++)
{
var dummy = Math.sqrt(i);
}
var end = + new Date();

alert(end - start);
```

Put a clock on your screen

The next example shows how to put a clock on your webpage. The setTimeout(function, 1000) is set to 1000 milliseconds, so you can see the seconds ticking away.

```
<!DOCTYPE html>
<html>
<body>
<h1 id="clock"></h1>
<script>
```

```
window.onload = starttime;
function starttime()
{
  var present = new Date();
  var hour   = present.getHours();
  var minute = present.getMinutes();
  var seconds = present.getSeconds();
  if (minute < 10) minute = "0" + minute;
  if (seconds < 10) seconds = "0" + seconds;
  document.getElementById("clock").innerHTML
        = "It is now " + hour + ":" + minute + ":"
+ seconds;
  setTimeout('starttime()', 1000);
}
</script>
</body>
</html>
```

Set a date to midnight

To set a date to midnight use the setHours() function in the following way.

```
var testdate;
testdate = new Date();
testdate.setHours(0,0,0,0);
alert(testdate);
```

With setHours() we set the time to 0 hours, 0 minutes, 0 seconds and 0 milliseconds

Show minutes always with two figures

The minutes in a date start with numbers containing just one figure (1, 2, 3 etc) If you need them to contain two figures you can add a leading 0 with padStart()

```
var mins = String(new
Date().getMinutes()).padStart(2, "0");
alert (mins)
```

Test if a date precedes another date

Using greater than (>), or smaller than (<), we can test if a date precedes another date. The next snippet shows how to do that.

```
var date1 = new Date(2021, 7, 31);
var date2 = new Date(2021, 8, 1);

if (date1 < date2)
{
alert ("date1 comes before date2");
}
```

Remember that months start counting at 0. Month 7 is therefore august.

Test if a date is in between two other dates

This snippet takes the previous one a step further. With this snippet we test if a day falls between two other dates. This can be used for example to test whether a hotel room is free in a certain time period.

```
var date1 = new Date(2021, 6, 10);
var date2 = new Date(2021, 6, 20);
var wanted = new Date(2021, 6, 15);

if ((wanted > date1) && (wanted < date2))
{
alert ("The room is free");
}
```

What day is it in x days

Say there is an event in 15 days, and you would like to know which day of the week that is. The next snippet shows how to get that information.

```
var futuredays = 8;
function nameofday(futuredays)
{
    var names=["sunday", "monday", "tuesday",
"wednesday", "thursday",
"friday","saturday","sunday"];
    var today = new Date().getDay();
    var future = futuredays % 7;
    return names[((today + future) % 7)];
};
alert(nameofday(futuredays));
```

Start by defining the variable futuredays and putting the number of days in the future in. Next, the array names is filled with the names of the weekdays. The variable today is set to the number of today's date. Because a week has seven days, we use the remains of the calculation of the number of days /7 to get to the right array element.

What day is it today

new Date gives us all the information about today. The first three letters give us the day of the week: mon, tue, wed,thu,fri,sat,sun We can use slice. to get the abbreviated day of the week.

```
var today = new Date();

today = today.toString();
alert (today)

var dayofweekweek = today.slice(0,3);
alert("Today is " + dayofweek);
```

What day is it today 2

To get the full name of the day you can use the next snippet:

```
var days = ['Sunday', 'Monday', 'Tuesday',
'Wednesday', 'Thursday', 'Friday', 'Saturday'];
var today = new Date();
var dayname = days[today.getDay()];
alert(dayname)
```

Change New Date() into any date you like or leave it empty for the current day.

What is todays date

The next snippet shows how to get todays date in the month-day-year format.

```
var current = new Date();
var day = String(current.getDate()).padStart(2,
'0');
var month = String(current.getMonth() +
1).padStart(2, '0');
var year = current.getFullYear();

current = month + "-" + day + "-" + year;
alert(current);
```

Which date is the most recent

To check which date of the two dates is the most recent, we just have to compare the two dates.

```
var date1;
var date2;
```

```
date1 = new Date( "Aug 31, 2020" );
date2 = new Date( "Dec 10, 2019" );

if (date1 > date2)
  {
  alert("The first date is the most recent");
  }
  else
  {
  alert("The second date is the most recent.");
  }
```

Which day in the year is it

If we need to know which day it is (aka how many days have passed since January 1) we can use the next snippet.

```
var milisecs = (new Date() - new Date(new
Date().getFullYear(), 0, 0))
var days = milisecs / 1000 / 60 / 60 / 24
alert (parseInt(days))
```

The first step is to subtract the first day of the year (new Date(new Date().getFullYear(), 0, 0) from the current day (new Date()). That gives us the total number of milliseconds and we then just have to divide that by the number of milliseconds in a day.

Which of the x days is the most recent

The next snippet shows how to get the most recent date from an array of dates.

```
var dates = [
  new Date(2021, 5, 12),
  new Date(2020, 7, 10),
```

```
   new Date(2021, 9, 9)
];

function mostrecent(...dates)
{
fulldate = new Date(Math.max(...dates));
recent = fulldate.getFullYear()+" :
"+fulldate.getMonth()+" : "+fulldate.getDate()
return recent
}

alert(mostrecent(...dates));
```

Which year is it

A simple snippet to determine which year it is.

```
var datenow = new Date();
var currentyear = datenow.getFullYear();
alert(currentyear);
```

Notes about date

108

Array

+ With an array concatenates

Using the + sign with an array might give some unpredictable results.

```
var value = ["a","b"] + ["c","d"]
alert(value);
alert(typeof value);
```

When you run this script, you will get the following results for value:
a, bc, d

This is also the case when using numbers

```
var value = [33, 55] + [10, 22];
alert(value);
alert(typeof value);
```

This will get the following result:

value will be: 33, 5510, 22
And value becomes a string.

A different way to address array elements

```
array = ["cellar", "Kitchen", "Livingroom",
"Mancave"]

alert(array.at(3))
```

The alert shows "Mancave" just like it would if you used alert(array[3])

Add an element to an array

Here is a simple method to add an element to an array.

```
var array = [1,2,3]
array = [...array, 5]
alert(array)
```

Add an element to an array at a predefined location

This snippet shows how to add an element to an array at a predefined place.

```
var testarray=['C++','Lua','Python']

testarray.splice(1,0,'Javascript')

alert(testarray)
```

splice inserts the new language at array index 1. The 0 in the splice command tells how many elements must be removed. In this case, we want to remove nothing, so the second value in the splice command is 0.

Add an element to an array only if it is new

The next snippet shows how to add an element to an array, but only if it is not already present in the array.

```
var array = ['test1','test2'];
var element = 'test2';

if(array.indexOf(element) === -1) {
    array.push(element);
}
```

Append an array to another array

If you want to append an array to another array, you can use the following snippet.

```
var a = [1,2,3];
var b = [4,5,6];

var c = a.concat(b);

alert (c);
```

In the example above a new array c[] is created. If you want to append array b to array a just use:

```
a = a.concat(b);
```

Append an array to another array 2

Javascript often provides multiple solutions leading to the same result. Here is another example to append two arrays. This time, the spread operator is used.

```
var a = [1,2,3];
var b = [4,5,6];

var c = [...a, ...b];

alert (c);
```

A new array (c) is constructed that contains all elements from array a and b.

If you want to append array a to array b just reverse the array names.

```
var c = [...b, ...a];
```

Append an array to another array 3

The command array.push() allows us to push variables into an array. It is not widely known that you can not only add variables but also complete arrays.

```
var languages = ['C++', 'Javascript']
var extra = ['Lua', 'Python']

languages.push(extra)

alert(languages)
```

Associative array

Normally, an array's elements are addressed by their index number.

```
var array=["Basic", "C++"]
alert (array[1])
```

You can however create array elements that use names as their index.

```
var learned=[]
learned["Basic"]="yes"
learned["C++"]="yes"
learned["Fortran"]="no"
alert(learned[1])
alert(learned["Basic"])
```

alert(learned[1]) will respond with "undefined"
alert(learned["Basic"]) will respond with "yes"

You can only address the array's elements with their name and not by index number.

Build a 2 dimensional array

Normally, we define the dimensions of an array. It is, however, possible to let Javascript build an array when we do not know the dimensions in advance.

```javascript
var testarray=[];
var row = 3;
var collumn = 3;
var count=0;

    for(i = 0; i < row; i++)
       {
       for(j = 0; j<collumn; j++)
          {
          if(!testarray[i])
            {
             testarray[i] = [];
            };
          count++;
          testarray[i][j] = count;
            };
       };

console.log(testarray);
```

We need to test in the for loop if testarray[i] exists. If not, it has to be created first before we can fill it. This example fills the array with 3 rows each with 3 columns, filled with the figures 1 to 9, by increasing the count value.

Check for double elements in an array

There is a simple method to test if there are double elements in an array. With a for loop, 'walk' through the array and test for each element if indexOf(element) is the same as lastIndexOf(element). If the first and last indexes are the same, then it is the same element.

```
var testarray = ["Luc", "Volders", 2021, "Luc"];

function nodoubles(){
    for(var i = 0; i < testarray.length; i++){
        var test = testarray[i];
        var firstIndex = testarray.indexOf(test);
        var lastIndex = testarray.lastIndexOf(test);
        if(firstIndex !== lastIndex){
            return false;
        };
    };
    return true;
};

alert(nodoubles(testarray));
```

The alert will show false in this example as my name occurs two times.

Check for double elements in an array 2

There are more ways to skin a cat and so has Javascript often multiple
solutions for a problem. We are going to test whether an array has double
elements but in a different way. Using new Set(array) we convert an array
into a set where the doubles are automatically removed. We can convert the
set back into an array with [...set]. Combining these two creates a new array
where the doubles have been removed. Now we only have to compare the
length of both arrays to see if the original one has doubles.

```
var test = ["Luc", "Volders", 2021, "Luc"];
var newtest = [...new Set(test)]
if (newtest.length !== test.length) {alert("there
are double elements")}
```

Convert an array with strings into an array with numbers

Here is a quick way to convert an array filled with strings into an array with numbers.

```
var stringarray = ["18", "20", "19"] ;
var numberarray = Array.from(stringarray, Number);
alert(numberarray);
```

A new array is created. If you do not want that, you can use the same array name:

```
var stringarray = Array.from(stringarray, Number);
```

Convert an array with strings into an array with numbers 2

An array with strings can be converted into an array with numbers with the map() function. Here is an example.

```
var array = ["1", "2", "3", "4"].map(i=>Number(i));
console.log(array);
```

Convert an array to only strings

Here is a simple method to convert an array to an array with only string elements.

```
var numbers = [ 1, 6, "a", 4, 8, "b", 5, 2];

numbers = numbers.map(String);

alert (typeof numbers[2]);
```

Convert an array with numbers into an array with strings

Here is a method to convert an array with numbers into an array with strings.

```
var numberarray = [18, 20, 19] ;
var stringarray = Array.from(numberarray, String);
alert(stringarray);
```

A new array is created. If you do not want that just use the same array.

```
var chain = [18, 20, 19] ;
var chain = Array.from(chain, String);
```

Convert an array to an CSV string

CSV files are often used for transferring data between programs with different file formats. Spreadsheets, for example, import CSV files. Using the next snippet, we can convert an array to an CSV string.

```
var temperatures = ["jan", 10.5, "feb", 16.3,
"mrt", 2.1];

var csvstring = temperatures.join(",");
alert(csvstring);
```

Convert an array to a string

Here is a quick way to convert an array into a string.

```
var testarray = [1, 2, 3, 4];
var teststring = testarray + "";
```

```
alert(teststring);
alert(typeof teststring);
```

This works also with multidimensional arrays and arrays with strings.

Convert an array to a string 2

Here is another method to convert an array to a string.

```
var myArray=['C++', 'Javascript', 'Python'];
var stringtest=myArray.join(' ');
alert(stringtest)
alert(typeof stringtest)
```

In this case myArray.join(' ') joins all the array elements in a string and puts spaces between them.

Convert an array into an object

The command Object.assign() makes it very easy to convert an array into an object. The next example shows how to use it.

```
var names = ['Basic', 'C++', 'Javascript', 'Lua'];

var obj = Object.assign({}, names);

console.log(obj);
```

Convert an array into an object 2

An easy method to convert an array into an object is to use the spread operator. Here is how it's done.

```
var names = ['Basic', 'C++', 'Javascript', 'Lua'];
objectnames={...names}
console.log(objectnames)
```

Copy an entire array

When we need a copy of an array we can do the following:

```
var testarray = [5, 6, 3, 4]
var copyarray = testarray
```

This might pose a problem as copyarray is not a full copy, but a list of memory addresses that refer to testarray. Therefore, any changes made in testarray will also be made in copyarray.

To prevent this, we can use 2 methods to make a full copy of an array:

```
var testarray = [5, 6, 3, 4];
var copyarray = testarray.slice();
```

The slice() command without any parameters uses the full array.

Another option is to use the spread operator:

```
var testarray = [5, 6, 3, 4];
var copyarray = [...testarray];
```

Copy part of an array

If you need to copy a known part of an array, you can use array.slice() as the next snippet shows.

```
var rooms = ["mancave", "attick", "living",
"garage"]
var part = rooms.slice(0,2)
```

```
alert(part)
```

Copy the positive elements from an array in a new array

We have an array filled with positive and negative numbers. We want to copy the positive values into a new array. The next snippet shows how.

```
var testarr = [87, -98, 3, -2, 123, -877, 22, -5,
23, -67]

var posarr = [];

for (var i=0; i<testarr.length; i++)
{
   if (testarr[i] >0)
      {
      posarr.push(testarr[i]);
      }
}
alert(posarr)
```

Start with building a new, empty array. Next iterate over the old array, and test each element if it it positive. If it is push() it into the new array.

Copy all even numbers into a new array

If you want to get all the even numbers from an array, and copy them into a new array, the next snippet shows how to do that.

```
var numbers = [1, 2, 3, 4, 5, 6, 7, 8, 9, 10, 11,
12];

var evenNumbers = numbers.filter(i => i %2 ==0 );
```

```
console.log(evenNumbers);
```

If you do not want to use arrow notation you can do it like this:

```
var numbers = [1, 2, 3, 4, 5, 6, 7, 8, 9, 10, 11,
12];

var evennumbers = numbers.filter(function(item) {
   return (item % 2 == 0);
});

console.log(evennumbers);
```

Count the unique items in an array

You might want to know how many unique items there are in an array. The following snippet makes an object from an array with the amount of unique items

```
var array = ["Javascript", "Python", "Javascript",
"C++"];
var unique = arr => {
   const count = {};
   for (var i = 0; i < array.length; i++) {
      count[arr[i]] = 1 + (count[arr[i]] || 0);
   };
   return count;
};

alert(JSON.stringify(unique(array)));
```

Alert wil show : { Javascript: 2, Python: 1, "C++": 1 }

Create an array with all the same elements

If you do not want empty elements when creating an array, you can use the next snippet.

```
var fillelements = 'Javascript tips -  ';
var testarray =
Array(3).fill(fillelements).join('');
alert (testarray);
```

The array is created with 3 elements, and each element is filled with the variable testarray.

Create an array and fill it with x unique numbers

The next snippet shows how to create an array with a predefined number of elements that are unique and random between 1 and 100. Change while(arr.length < 10) in the number of elements you need, and change Math.floor(Math.random() * 50) in the highest number you need.

```
var array = [];
while (array.length < 10) {
    var r = Math.floor(Math.random() * 50) + 1;
    if (array.indexOf(r) === -1) array.push(r);
}
console.log(arr);
```

Delete clears an element

When you use delete to remove an element from an array, the length of the array does not change. The element is cleared but not removed.

```
var testarray = [ "one", "two", "three", "four"];
```

```
delete testarray[2];
alert (testarray);
```

The alert will show "one", "two", ,"four"

The command delete clears the element but does not remove it. The array now contains one empty element. This can be an advantage as the array's index does not alter.

Empty an array

The easiest and fastest way to empty an array is shown by the next snippet.

```
var testarray = [0, 1, 2, 3, 4, 5, 6, 7, 8, 9];
testarray.length = 0;
```

Exchange two array elements

If you need to exchange two array elements, the easiest way to do that is using destructuring like the following snippet shows.

```
var testarray = ['javascript', 'c++'];

[testarray[0], testarray[1]] = [testarray[1],
testarray[0]];

console.log(testarray)
```

Exchange two array elements 2

If you need to swap two array elements, you can do that with a helper variable. Here is an example.

```
var helper = array[y];
array[y] = array[x];
array[x] = helper;
```

Exchange array elements from different arrays

This tip uses the same method as the tip where two array elements are
exchanged. The difference is that we here exchange elements from 2
different arrays.

```
var testarray = ['javascript', 'c++'];
var testarray2 = ["python", "lua"];

[testarray[0], testarray2[0]] = [testarray2[0],
testarray[0]];

console.log(testarray)
console.log(testarray2)
```

The output will be:
['python', 'c++']
['javascript', 'lua']

Fill an array with numbers from a starting value up to a maximum

To fill an empty array with values starting at a certain number up to a
maximum number, we can use the following snippet:

```
var testarray = [];
var start = 90;
var maximum = 100-start;

for( var i=1; testarray.push(start + i++) <
maximum;) ;
```

Fill an array with the numbers 0 till a maximum value

Here is an easy way to fill an array with the numbers from 0 to x. Just use the keys like this:

```
Array.from(Array(10).keys())
```

In this example the array will have the following contents [0,1,2,3,4,5,6,7,8,9]

Filter even numbers from an array

The next snippet shows a function that filters the even numbers out of an array.

```
var array = [-3, -2, -1, 1, 2, 3];

var evennrs = array.filter(function(x) {
    return x % 2 === 0;
})

console.log(evennrs);
```

Filter negative values from an array

You can use the filter command to remove negative numbers from an array. The next snippet shows how.

```
var array = [18, -42, 21, 6, -50];
array = array.filter(larger => larger > -1);
console.log(array);
```

If you do not want to use the arrow notation you can use the normal function syntax like this:

```
var array = [18, -42, 21, 6, -50];
array = array.filter(function(x) { return x >
-1; });
console.log(array);
```

Filter values from an array

The command filter() is an easy way to filter values out of an array. The
next example creates a new array with only words from the old array that
are longer than 3 letters.

```
var languages = ['C++', 'Basic', 'Javascript',
'Lua', 'Python'];

var result = languages.filter(word => word.length >
3);

alert(result);
```

The next line filters the word "Lua" from the same array

```
var result = languages.filter(word => word !=
"Lua");
```

Find an element in an array

Using array.includes() is a fast method to check whether an array contains
an element. Use it like this:

```
var testarray = ["aaa", "bbb", "ccc"]

if (testarray.includes("bbb"))
{
alert("bbb is found in the array");
}
```

To find where the wanted value is in the array, you can use the following code:

```
where=testarray.indexOf("bbb");
alert(where);
```

Find an object in an array

If you need to search for a certain object in an array with objects, this is an easy method to do so.

```
var arr = [
    { name:"little", lang1:"Basic", lang2: "Lua" },
    { name:"much", lang1:"Javascript", lang2:
"Python" }
            ];

var found = arr.find(test => test.name === 'much');

console.log(found);
```

In this example, we search for an object with the key name "much"

Find the missing numbers in an integer array

Imagine an array filled with integer numbers and, some numbers are missing. The next snippet shows how to find the missing numbers.

```
var array = [11,12,15,17];
start = 10;
end = 20;
missing = [];

for (let i = start; i <= end+1; i++)
{
```

```
  if (array.indexOf(i) === -1)
  {
    missing.push(i)
  }
}
console.log(missing)
```

Flatten an array

If you need to make a single dimensional array from a multidimensional array (flatten the array), there are two methods available. You can use array = array.flat() or array =[].concat(...array). To demonstrate these, here is a snippet that shows how to use these commands.

```
var arr = ["Javascript", "Python", ["Basic",
"Lua"]];

array = arr.flat();
alert(array)
```

Or you can use:

```
array = [].concat(...arr)
alert(array)
```

Functions inside an array

We can put a function inside an array element. De function can then be called with: arrayname[index](). Here is a snippet that demonstrates this.

```
var a=5;
var b=6;

var array_of_functions =
[
```

```
    function() { c=a*b; return c },
    function() { alert('a string') },
    function() { alert('another string') },
    function() { alert('the third string') }
]

d=array_of_functions[0]();
alert(d);
array_of_functions[1]();
```

In this script alert(d) will call the function in the first array element (0) and answer the result which is 30. array_of_functions[1]() will call the function in array element [1] The functions are executed because of the () after the array element.

Get a random element from an array

If we need to pick a random element from an array filled with names, data, or other values we can do that with the following script.

```
function chosename(names)
{
    const randomnumber = Math.floor(Math.random() *
names.length);
    return names[randomnumber];
}

names = ["Javascript", "C++", "Python", "Lua",
"Basic"];
alert(chosename(names));
```

Get an element from the end of an array

To get the last element from an array you can use array.slice(-1)

```
var array = [10, 20, 30, 40, 50];
document.write(array.slice(-1));
```

Using array.slice(-3) will get the last 3 elements.

```
var array = [10, 20, 30, 40, 50];
document.write(array.slice(-3));
```

A new array is made that contains only the last three elements of the original one.

When you just need the third-last element from an array, you can do that with the following snippet.

```
var array = [10, 20, 30, 40, 50];
document.write(array.slice(-3)[0]);
```

Get the diagonal elements out of an array

If we have a multi dimensional array and we need the values of the diagonal elements we can do that with a for loop. We therefore need to increase the values of the x and y co-ordinates at the same time. This can be done by using the comma operator in the for declaration.

```
var testarray = [
[1,2,3],
[4,5,6],
[7,8,9]
];

alert(testarray);

var x=0;
var y=0;

for(x = 0,y = 0; x < testarray.length; x++, y++)
{
alert(testarray[x][y]);
```

}

This shows how the x and y values are increased in the for loop at the same time. The alert shows the values 1, 5 and 9

Get the elements that occur in two arrays

The next snippet shows how to get elements out of two arrays that only occur in one of these arrays.

```
var testarray1 = [1,1,2,3,4,4];
var testarray2 = [1,3,4,5,8];
var newarray1 = Array.from(new Set(testarray1));
var newarray2 = Array.from(new Set(testarray2));

var result = newarray1.filter(item =>
newarray2.includes(item));
alert(result);
```

Get elements that occur in an array but not in an other array

By changing just one thing in the previous snippet, we can test which elements are found in array 1, that do not occur in array 2.

```
var testarray1 = [1,1,2,3,4,4];
var testarray2 = [1,3,4,5,8];
var newarray1 = Array.from(new Set(testarray1));
var newarray2 = Array.from(new Set(testarray2));

var result = newarray1.filter(item => !
newarray2.includes(item));
alert(result);
```

We only have to change newarray2.includes(item) in

!newarray2.includes(item)

Get the last element of an array

Use array.length-1 as the index to obtain the last element of an array.

```
var testarray = ["jan", "feb", "mar", "apr"];
var last = testarray[testarray.length-1];
alert(last)
```

Get the last element out of an array

The next snippet shows how to get the last element from an array. The element is also removed from the array.

```
var array = [1, 2, 3, 4, 5, 6, 7, 8];
var last = arr.pop();

console.log(array);
console.log(last);
```

Get the last x elements out of an array

The previous tip showed how to get the last element out of an array. Another method to get the last element is to use array.slice(-1). We can also use this to get the last x elements out of an array.

```
var a;
var b;
var c;
var testarray = [0, 1, 2, 3, 4, 5, 6, 7] ;
[a, b, c]= testarray.slice(-3);
```

```
alert(b);
```

The above snippet shows how to get the last 3 elements out of an array and at the same time put them into 3 new elements using array destructuring.

Get the lowest and highest values in an array

We can sort an array to find the lowest and highest values, but this alters the array itself. To find the lowest and highest values without altering the array, use the following snippet:

```
var numbers = ["1", "2", 1.5, 6.7];
var max = Math.max(...numbers);
var min = Math.min(...numbers);

alert("Lowest = " + min + " Highest = " + max)
```

Javascript code in an array element

You can put almost anything in an array. Here is an example that puts code in an array and then makes that code work by using eval.

```
var i;
var text = "";

var array1 = [
5,
6,
"hello 1 " ,
"hello 2" ,
'for (i = 0; i < array1.length-1; i++) {text +=
array1[i] + "<br>";}'
];

var test = array1[4];
```

```
document.write(eval(test));
```

Move an element in an array to a new index

To move an element in an array to a new position, we first remove the
element, and then put it in its new place with array.splice(). Here is how to
do that.

```
var array = [ "Lua", "Basic", "C++", "Javascript",
"Python"]

var location = array.splice(0,1);
array.splice(3,0, location);
alert(array)
```

First, we remove the element at location 0 and put it in the variable location.
The array then looks like Basic, C++, Javascript, Python. Then we put the
variable location at the 4th position in the array.

Move an element to the first location in an array

If you want to move an element from somewhere inside the array, to the
first location, then you can do that with array.splice() and array.unshift().
Here is an example.

```
var array = ["C++", "Javascript", "Lua","Basic",
"Python"]
var position = 3;
array.unshift(array.splice(position, 1)[0]);
alert(array)
```

Optimizing array loops

We often have to iterate through an array without knowing the length of the array. We can get the length with array.length but this value is calculated every time:

```
var testarray = [ 15,8,9,12,7,6];
var i;
for (i = 0; i<testarray.length; i++)
{
document.write(testarray[i] + " ");
}
```

In this program, the loop has to test every time whether i is less than testarray.length. Using this with a small array like the one above is not a big issue. When using this in an array with 1000's of elements, this slows the iteration down. It is much faster to calculate array.length once and put it in a separate variable, which we will use to iterate the array.

```
var testarray = [ 15,8,9,12,7,6];
number = testarray.length
var i;
for (i = 0; i<number; i++)
{
document.write(testarray[i]+" ");
}
```

Process two arrays of different length

To process two arrays with different lengths we need to work with the shortest length to not get into trouble. In the next example, we add the elements of two arrays which have different lengths. The solution is a new array with the length of the shortest array.

```
var shortarray = [1, 2, 3, 4, 5];
var longarray = [3, 6, 9, 2, 1, 8, 7, 3];
var additionarray = [];
```

```
for (var i = 0; i < Math.min(shortarray.length,
longarray.length); i++)
    {
       additionarray[i] = arr[i] + arr1[i];
    }

alert(additionarray);
```

Math.min(shortarray.length, langarray.length) makes sure that the loop processes only as much elements that are present in the shortest array.

Put the array elements in a random sequence

Often arrays are sorted. If you want to put the elements of an array in a random sequence, you can use the following snippet.

```
var testarray = [0,1,2,3,4,5,6,7,8,9];

function randomise(array) {
  var i, j, temp;
  for (i = array.length - 1; i > 0; i--) {
    j = Math.floor(Math.random() * (i + 1));
    temp = array[i];
    array[i] = array[j];
    array[j] = temp;
  }
  return array;
}

alert(randomise(testarray));
```

Put the array elements in a random sequence 2

We can shuffle array elements with the following snippet.

138

```
var testarray = [0,1,2,3,4,5,6,7,8,9];
testarray.sort(function()
{
    return Math.random() - .5
});
alert(testarray);
```

Que Simulation

A que is a lineup. Compared to real life a lineup is first come, first served.
Queues are sometimes used in programs, and they are called on a First-In-
First-Out basis (FIFO). This can easily be achieved by creating an array and
using the array functions array.push() and array.shift()

```
var que = [];
var vara;

function inque(data)
{
que.push(data);
}

function fromque()
{
return que.shift();
}
```

Two functions are created: inque() which puts data into the que, and
fromque() which removes the first in line. This can be shortened with arrow
notation:

```
inque=(data)=>que.push(data);
fromque=()=>que.shift();
```

We can use the que, by calling the functions with a parameter:

```
inque(6);
inque(5);
```

```
inque(3);
alert("the que contains now " + que);

vara = fromque();
alert("First In First Out " + vara);
alert("remains   " + que);
```

Reverse an array

To reverse an array you simply use: array.reverse(). If you want to keep the original array intact you can define a new array while reversing it like this:

```
var array=[1,2,3,4,5,6]
var newarray = array.reverse()
alert(newarray)
```

Reversing an array

When you need to reverse an array, the easiest method is to use array.reverse() This however does not make a new array but reverses the original one.

To reverse an array into a new array you can use the following solution:

```
var testarray = [1, 2, 3, 4, 5];
testarray2 = testarray.slice().reverse();
alert(testarray2);
alert("testarray 2 : " + testarray2);
testarray2[1]=7;
alert("testarray : " + testarray);
```

When running this script, you will see that testarray and testarry2 are completely different arrays, and changing a value in one of them will not affect the other one.

Remove and modify array elements with one command

With array splice(x,y), we can remove items from an array starting at location x and remove y items.

Less known is that we can add parameters to replace the removed elements with new ones. You can do that as follows:

```
var task = ["We", "are", "starting", "programming",
"tomorrow"];

task.splice(0, 4, "I", "am", "going", "to", "buy",
"Javascript", "tips");

console.log(task);
```

Notice that we removed 4 elements and added 7 elements.

Remove duplicates from an array

If you want to clean up an array by removing duplicates, the following snippet shows an easy solution.

```
var array = ["a", "a", "b", "c", "c", "d", "e"];
array = [...new Set(array)];
alert (array);
```

This works with arrays with text, numbers and mixed types.

In the above example, the original array is altered. If you want to keep the original array and have a new array in which the duplicates are removed, the solution is simple: just give it another name:

```
var array = ["a", "a", "b", "c", "c", "d", "e"];
newarray = [...new Set(array)];
alert (newarray);
```

Remove duplicates from two arrays

If you want to combine two arrays into one and remove the duplicates, this is how you can do that:

```
var first = ["Javascript", "Lua", "Python"];
var second = ["C++", "Basic", "Lua", "Python"];
var new2= [...first, ...second];
var new3=[...new Set(new2)]
alert(new3)
```

First, we combine the two arrays into one with the ...spread operator. Then we remove the double entries with the new Set command.

Remove double entries from an array

There is a special kind of array called a set. A set does not accept double entries. So the easiest method to remove double entries out from an array is to convert the array into a set and then convert it back to an array. The next snippet shows how to do that.

```
var testarray = ["Javascript", "tips", "tips",
"Luc", "Luc", "Volders"];
var nodoubles = Array.from(new Set(testarray));
alert(nodoubles);
```

Another way is to use the spread (...) operator like this:

```
var testarray = ["Javascript", "tips", "tips",
"Luc", "Luc", "Volders"];
var nodoubles = [...new Set(testarray)];
alert(nodoubles);
```

Remove elements from an array

splice is used to remove elements from an array. splice accepts two parameters. The first one is the index where to start, and the second one is the number to be removed. Please be aware that counting starts at 0.

```
array = [1, 2, 3, 4, 5, 6, 7, 8, 9]

var begin = 2;
var number = 3;

arr.splice(begin, number);

alert(arr)
```

This example removes the figures 3,4 and 5. Removing starts at element 2, which is figure 3 as we start counting at 0, and removes 2 elements.

Remove falsey values from an array

Here is a simple solution for removing falsey (0, undefined, null, false) values from an array.

```
var testarray = ["a", "test", 150 ,225 ,233,
undefined, 4, false, ""]

var testarray = testarray.filter(Boolean);

console.log(testarray);
```

The array wil now contain: ['a', 'test', 150, 225, 233, 4]

Just be carefull because this also removes 0.

Remove one or more elements from an array

There is an array that contains the next elements:

```
var testarray =
[ "jan","feb","mar","apr","may","jun"];
```

If we want to remove "mar" from the array, we have to know its location. In this case, that is 2. To remove "mar" from the array, we can use the following command:

```
array.splice(2, 1);
```

This removes 1 element at location 2.

If we do not know the location but know that we want to remove the value "apr" we can use the following lines:

```
var toberemoved = "apr";
for(var i = testarray.length - 1; i >= 0; i--)
    {
    if(testarray[i] === toberemoved)
      {
       testarray.splice(i, 1);
      }
    }
```

The array is iterated, and a test is performed that compares each element with the variable to be removed. If a match is found, the element is removed.

In the above example, the array is shortened with 1 element. There are only five elements left in the array, and that can influence other parts of your program. If you do not want the array to have fewer elements you can empty the location in the array. In that case replace testarray.splice(i, 1); by:

```
delete array[i];
```

The array will then be as follows:
["jan","feb","mar",,"may","jun"];

144

Now we have an array with an empty element in it. This element contains "undefined" which is something that is not desirable in all cases. If you do not want empty elements in your array, you can replace "apr" by a special character like "*". To achieve that, use, in stead of testarray.splice(i, 1); the following line:

```
testarray[i]="*";
```

Remove the first x elements from an array

Using array.slice(x ,1) we can remove the element with index x from the array. But if we use array.slice(x) this will remove the first x elements from the array. The next snippet gives an example.

```
var array = [1,2,3,4,5]
array=array.slice(2)
alert(array) // => [3, 4, 5]
```

Remove the last x elements from an array

To remove the last x elements from an array you can use the next snippet.

```
var testarray = [0, 1, 2, 3, 4, 5, 6, 7, 8, 9];
testarray = testarray.slice(0,6);

alert(testarray);
```

Because there are only 6 elements left in the array, alert displays the numbers 0 to 6 (excluding).

Remove the last x elements from an array 2

Here is another method to remove the last x elements from an array.

```
var testarray = [0, 1, 2, 3, 4, 5, 6, 7, 8, 9];
testarray.length = 6;

alert(testarray);
```

Because there are only 6 elements left in the array, alert displays the numbers 0 to 6 (excluding).

Rorate the last array element to the front

To move the last array element to the front, use array.pop() to first remove it from the back, and array.unshift() to push it into the front.

```
var testarr = [1,2,3,4];
var testarr.unshift(testarr.pop())
alert(testarr)
```

Rotate the first array element to the back

To move the first array element to the back, it has to be removed with array.shift() and pushed at the back with array.push().

```
var testarr = [1,2,3,4];
var testarr.push(testarr.shift())
alert(testarr)   // =>2,3,4,1
```

Remove the second last element from an array

To remove the second last element from an array, use this snippet:

```
var array = [1,2,3,4]
var seclast = array.splice(array.length -2,1)
alert(seclast)
```

Search a string in a multidimensional array

We can search a string inside an array with includes(). However this does not work in a multi dimensional array like the next example shows.

```
var names = ['Basic', 'Python', ['C++',
'Javascript', ['Lua']]];
alert(names.includes("Lua"));
```

The alert shows "false", as includes() does not work inside a multi-dimensional array.

The solution is to flatten the array with JSON.stringify, and then search for the string.

```
var names = ['Basic', 'Python', ['C++',
'Javascript', ['Lua']]];

function isinside(names,lookfor)
{
return JSON.stringify(names).includes(lookfor);
}

trueornot = isinside(names,"Lua");
alert(trueornot);
```

Now the alert shows "true"

Search an item in an array

There are several ways to search items in an array. The method presented here is to use the filter() function. The next snippet demonstrates this.

```
var languages = ["Basic", "C++", "Javascript",
"Lua", "Python"];

var search = (lookfor, source) =>
{
  var query = lookfor.toLowerCase();
  return source.filter(item =>
item.toLowerCase().indexOf(query) >= 0);
}

console.log(search("as", languages));
```

This example searches for the letters "as" in the array languages, and finds Basic and Javascript.

Search and remove an item

The next snippet shows how to search and remove an item from an array. The element is searched with indexOf() and at the same time removed with slice()

```
var testarray = ["jan", "feb", "march", "apr", "may"];
testarray.splice (testarray.indexOf("apr"), 1);
```


Shuffle the array elements

If you need to mix the elements in an ordered array, you can use the following command:

```
array.sort(() => Math.random() - 0.5);
```

If you do not want to use the arrow notation, you can use this:

```
array.sort(function() { return 0.5 -
Math.random() });
```

Skip array elements with destructuring

While converting an array to variables, with the destructering method, you can skip array elements like this.

```
var array = ['Basic', 'C++', 'Javascript'];

var [x, , z] = array;

console.log(x);
console.log(z);
```

Sort a multidimensional array

A two-dimensional array can be sorted by its index

```
var array = [[12, 'AAA'], [12, 'BBB'], [12, 'CCC'],
[28, 'DDD'], [18, 'CCC'],[12, 'DDD'],[18, 'CCC'],
[28, 'DDD'],[28, 'DDD'],[58, 'BBB'],[78, 'BBB']];

array.sort(function(a,b) {
    return a[0]-b[0]
});
```

In this example, we sort on index [0] which are the numbers. If you want to sort on the second index (the words), use this code:

```
return (a[1] < b[1]) ? -1 : 1;
```

Sort a two dimensional array on the second element

To sort a two dimensional array on it's second element, use the next code:

```
var array = [[1, "Javascript"], [2, "Basic"], [3,
"Lua"], [4, "C++"]];

array.sort(function (a, b) {
    return a[1]>(b[1]);
});

alert(array)
```

Sort an array according to the length of its elements

To sort an array according to the length of its elements, you can use the next snippet.

```
var textar = ["Python", "Javascript", "C++"];
function sortonlength()
   {
   var sorted = textar.sort(function(a, b)
   {
       return a.length - b.length;
   })
   return sorted;
};
alert(sortonlength(textar));
```

Sort an array by the dates in the elements

You can sort an array with numbers, letters, strings, etc. But you can also sort an array by the dates in it.

```
array.sort((a,b) =>  new Date(b.date) - new
Date(a.date));
```

Sort an array case insensitive

When sorting an array where strings are present starting with a capital letter
and strings without a capital letter, the strings starting with a capital letter
will get first.

```
var names = ['C', 'javascript', 'Java',
"python",'Lua', 'basic'];
names.sort();
alert(names)
```

alert will show: C,Java,Lua,basic,javascript,python

Obviously that is not what we want. We want the array to be in
alphabetical order. Use the next piece of code to achieve this.

```
var names = ['C', 'javascript', 'Java',
"python",'Lua', 'basic'];

names.sort(function (a, b)
   {
     var a = a.toUpperCase();
     var b = b.toUpperCase();

     return (a === b) ? 0 : a > b ? 1 : -1;
   });
alert(names);
```

Sort an array with numbers

I presume this tip is well known; nevertheless, I did not want to leave it out.

To sort an array the sort() command is used. Unfortunately it does not sort arrays with numbers well.

```
[0, 11, 5, 25, 2, 125, 3].sort();
```

This brings us : [0, 11, 125, 2, 25, 3,   5]

The sort command sorts alphabetically not numeric.

The solution is to use a function with a comparator in the sort command.

```
var numberarray =[0, 11, 5, 25, 2, 125, 3];

numberarray.sort(function(a,b) {return a-b});
alert (numberarray);
```

This time it sorts like we want: [0, 2, 3, 5, 11, 25, 125]

Sort an array descending

To sort an array we normally use the compare function (a-b).
To sort an array descending we only have to change this in (b-a).

```
var numbers = [ 1, 6, 4, 8, 5, 2];

numbers.sort(function(a,b) {return b-a});
alert (numbers);
```

Sorting an array while creating a new array

When we sort an array with the array.sort method, the array itself is sorted.
What if we want the array in its original form and a sorted version.
As you will know arrays are Objects in Javascript. So if we duplicate an array, it is not a new array but a reference to the original one. For example:

152

```
var proglangs = ['Python','Javascript','C+
+','Lua'];
var sortproglangs = proglangs;
sortproglangs = sortproglangs.sort();
alert(proglangs);
alert(sortproglangs);
sortproglangs.push("Basic");
alert(proglangs);
alert(sortproglangs);
```

Adding one element to one of the arrays adds that element also to its copy.

If we do not want this to happen, we have to make sure that the copy is indeed a new array. This can be done with slice()

```
var proglangs = ['Python','Javascript','C+
+','Lua'];
var sortproglangs = proglangs.slice();
sortproglangs = sortproglangs.sort();
alert(proglangs);
alert(sortproglangs);
proglangs.push("Basic");
alert("proglangs after adding : "+proglangs);
alert("sortproglangs after adding :
"+sortproglangs);
```

Sorting an array while creating a new array using JSON

This is a variation on the previous tip. We want to sort an array resulting in a new array, and at the same time keeping the original.

```
var proglang = ['Python','Javascript','C++','Lua'];
var sortproglang =
JSON.parse(JSON.stringify(proglang));
sortproglang = sortproglang.sort();
alert(proglang);
alert(sortproglang);
```

In this version the original array is converted to a JSON string, from which a new array is made. The new array is no longer just a reference to the old one.

Sort an array so that odd numbers come first

If you need to sort an array in such a way that the odd values are in the front indexes, use the following code:

```
var array=[314,1,2,3,575,4,5,6]
array.sort((a,b)=>{
   if (a%2==b%2) return a-b;
   if (a%2>b%2) return -1;
   return 1;
})
console.log(array)
```

Sort an array that includes sub-arrays

Here is an array filled with sub-arrays that contain the temperature per month. If you want to sort such an array based on the temperature value, here is the method to do that.

```
var temperatures =
   [
       ["Jan", 5],
       ["Feb", 7],
       ["Jul", 25],
       ["Aug", 23],
       ["Okt", 18]
   ];

temperatures.sort(function(a,b) {return a[1]-
b[1]});
```

```
console.log(temperatures);
```

The result will be:

```
[
  [ 'Jan', 5 ],
  [ 'Feb', 7 ],
  [ 'Okt', 18 ],
  [ 'Aug', 23 ],
  [ 'Jul', 25 ]
]
```

Sort an array with objects on a property

Using array.sort(function (a,b){}) ables us to sort an array alphabetically. However, this is not possible if the array is filled with objects. The next snippet shows how to sort an array with objects based on one of the objects properties.

```
var temps = [
  {id: 1, month: "jan", rain: 0},
  {id: 2, month: "feb", rain: 2},
  {id: 3, month: "mrt", rain: 8},
  {id: 4, month: "apr", rain: 6},
  {id: 5, month: "may", rain: 10},
  {id: 6, month: "jun", rain: 5},
]

function compare(a, b)
{
  var rain1 = a.rain;
  var rain2 = b.rain;
  var comp = 0;
  if (rain1 > rain2) {
    comp = 1;
  } else if (rain1 < rain2) {
    comp = -1;
  }
```

```
    return comp;
}
```

```
temps.sort(compare)
```

```
document.write(JSON.stringify(temps))
```

In this example the array is sorted on the property rain. Changing a.rain and b.rain in a.month and b.month the array gets alphabetically sorted on the property month. If we use a.id and b.id the array will get sorted on the property id.

If you like arrow notations then you can replace the above function with the next line:

```
temps.sort((a,b) => (a.rain > b.rain) ? 1 :
((b.rain > a.rain) ? -1 : 0));
```

Sort an array depending on values of another array

Suppose you have an array with sorted elements. And there is another array with the elements mixed up. You want to sort the mixed up array in the same manner as the sorted array. Here is an example that shows how you can do that.

```
var all = ["Basic", "C++", "Javascript", "Lua",
"Python"]
```

```
var test = ["Javascript", "Basic"]
```

```
test.sort(function(a,b)
    {
    return all.indexOf(a) - all.indexOf(b);
    })
alert(test)
```

The alert shows: Basic,Javascript

You can use this for example, to sort an array with mixed up months, in the right order.

Sort an array with words with accents

Foreign words often have accents. Sorting an array with these words will not succeed. To sort it the right way, use localeCompare() in your sort function. Here is an example.

```
var words = ["café", "rosé", "scène", "etagère",
"être", "gêne"];

words.sort();
alert("Normal sort without using localeCompare : "
+ words);

words.sort(function(a, b){return
a.localeCompare(b)});
alert("Sorting using localeCompare : " + words);
```

Split an array in half

The next snippet shows how to split an array in half and put the contents in two new arrays.

```
var array = [1, 2, 3, 4, 5, 6]
var mid = Math.ceil(array.length / 2);

var firstpart = array.splice(0, mid)
var secondpart = array.splice(-mid)

alert(firstpart)
alert(secondpart)
```

Split an array in parts

Using slice() we can split an array into parts. In the next example we split an array at the third element, and put the first and second part in separate arrays.

```
var array = [0,1,2,3,4,5];

var arr1 = array.slice(0,3);
var arr2 = array.slice(3);

alert(arr1);
alert(arr2);
```

Stack creation

If you are familiar with Machine language programming, you know there is a special kind of storage called a stack. A stack is build on Last-In-First-Out functionality. It is a kind of pile where you put things on top of eachtother and you can only take the top item away. We can easily build a stack with an array and then use the array.push() and array.pop commands.

```
var stack = [];
var vara;

function instack(data)
{
stack.push(data);
}

function fromstack()
{
return stack.pop();
}
```

Or even shorter with arrow notation:

```
instack=(data)=>stack.push(data);
fromstack=()=>stack.pop();
```

Two functions are created. The first has the name instack() and we use this
to push data on the stack. The second has the name from.stack() and
retrieves (and removes) the last element put on the stack. You can use them
as follows:

```
instack(10);
instack(5);
alert(stack);

vara = fromstack();
alert(vara);
```

Sum the elements in an array

Suppose you have an array that contains the order of a customer.
Alternating elements contain a name and the price. To add all prices, you
can use the next example.

```
var order = ["ESP32 Simplified", 19.95, 'Javascript
tips', 19.95];

    var total = 0;
    for(var i = 0; i < order.length; i++)
      {
      var price = order[i];
      if(+price)
        {
          total += +price;
        };
      };

console.log(total);
```

Test if a value occurs in an array

Using array.includes() it is easy to test if a value or text occurs in the array.

```
var languages = ["Javascript", "Lua", "Python"]

var testlang = languages.includes("Basic")
alert(testlang)

The alert will show "false"
```

Test if a value occurs in an array 2

We can test if a value or text occurs in an array with the clever use of array.indexOf(). Here is how to perform the test.

```
var languages = ["Javascript", "Lua", "Python"]

if(languages.indexOf("Basic") == -1)
  {
    alert("The language Basic is not present")
  }
```

array.indexOf(variable) will point to the index if the variable is present, and otherwise it will have the value -1.

Test if an array has empty elemenrs

To test if an array has empty elements we can use myArray.every(element => element !== "") You can replace the "" by any other string or element if you need to search for something else. The next snippet shows an example on how you can use this.

```
testarray = ["a", "b", "", "d"]
```

```
if (testarray.every(element => element !== ""))
   {
   alert ("no empty elements");
   }
   else
   {
   alert("found some empty elements");
   }
```

Test if an array is empty

You might define an empty array at the start of your program. The next lines of code show how to test later on if the array is (still) empty

```
array = []

if (typeof array !== 'undefined' && array.length
=== 0)
{
    alert("no elements in array")
}
```

Test if an element exists and give the next one in line

In this example, there are courses in programming languages you need to follow. When you have finished a course you need to do the next. The languages are array elements. The finished course is put into a variable. The following function supplies the next course you must follow.

```
var languages = ["Basic", "Python", "Javascript",
"C++"];

function nextcourse(lookfor,languages)
{
    found = languages.indexOf(lookfor) + 1;
```

```
        return languages[found] || "All done";
}
document.write(nextcourse('Javascript',
languages));
document.write("<br>");
document.write(nextcourse('Lua', languages));
```

If the variable contains a language that is not in the list (like Lua), then the array index will be -1, and the function takes the first index which is Basic. When all courses have been taken, and the variable contains C++ then the value of found will become 4. This is a non-existent index and the || will be chosen which displays "All Done"

Test whether a variable is present in a flat array

If we just need a quick check whether a variable is present in a flat array, we can use the next code in arrow-notation:

```
var testarray = ["a", "b", "c", "d"];

var isinarray =(value) =>
testarray.includes(value);

testvar = "b";
alert(isinarray(testvar));
```

We test for the value "b" and the alert will say true.

Test if two array's are equal

To test whether two arrays are equal, convert them first to strings and then test for equality like the next sample shows.

```
var first = [1, 2, 3, 4, 5];
var second = [1, 2, 3, 4, 5];
```

```
var equal = first.toString() === second.toString();
alert(equal);
```

Test if two arrays are equal 2

To test whether two arrays are equal, it is not possible to use (first ==
second). The comparison == does not test nested (multidimensional) arrays.
A different method than the one mentioned in the previous tip is to use
JSON.stringify as the next snippet shows.

```
var first = [1, 2, 3, 4, 5, ["a", "b"]];
var second = [1, 2, 3, 4, 5, ["a", "b"]];

alert(JSON.stringify(first)==JSON.stringify(second)
);
```

Test if two arrays contain the same elements

The previous tip tested if sortedb arrays are equal. By sorting
the elements, we can test if the arrays elements are equal.

```
var first = [1, 2, 3, 4, 5];
var second = [1, 2, 3, 4, 5];
var equal = first.toString().sort ===
second.toString().sort;
alert(equal);
```

Test whether an array contains the elements of another array

The next snippet shows a fast way to test whether all the elements of an
array are present in another array.

```
var array1 = ["C++", "Java", "Javascript", "Lua",
"Python"];
var array2 = ["Javascript", "Lua", "Python"];
var present = array2.every((item) =>
array1.includes(item));
alert(present)
```

Test whether an array contains the elements of another array 2

Here is another method to check if the elements of an array exist in another array. The difference from the previous method is that the original array is two dimensional.

```
var micros = [["Arduino", "ESP8266"], ["ESP8266",
"ESP32"], ["Arduino","Raspberry Pico"]];

function search(wanted, micros)
{
    return !!micros.find(micros => micros.join() ===
wanted.join());
}

alert(search(["Arduino","ESP32"], micros));
alert(search(["ESP8266", "ESP32"], micros));
```

Three methods to iterate over an array with a for loop

There are three ways to iterate over an array with a for loop, to look for a certain value or to change values. Here are examples that use the three methods to get the same result.

```
var testarray = [3, 5, 7, 9, 11];
```

```
for (i=0; i<testarray.length; i++)
{
    if (testarray[i] == 7)
    {
      console.log("found");
    }
}
```

Method 2:

```
for (var index in testarray)
{
        if (testarray[index] == 7)
    {
        console.log("found");
    }
}
```

Method 3:

```
for (var element of testarray)
{
  if (element == 7)
    {
        console.log("found");
    }
}
```

The first for loop is the traditional method in which we determine the length of the array and use that to walk through all its elements to find the value 7.

The second for loop uses the word "in" to automatically determine the length and uses the variable index to walk through the elements.

The third loop uses "of" to walk through the elements. The length is automatically detected, and the index value is not used. The for-of combination walks automatically through all elements.
Which one to use depends on the purpose of the loop and your personal preferences.

165

Universal array sorter

In the tip where I showed how to sort an array with words that have accents, there is one problem. That function will not sort numbers. So here is a universal array sort routine, that sorts strings, strings with accents, and numbers.

```
var figures = [3, 10, 2, 14, 7, 2, 9, 5];
var words = ["café", "rosé", "scène", "etagère",
"être", "gêne"];

function sortall(a, b)
{
    if (a < b)
    {
        return -1;
    }
    else if (a > b)
    {
        return 1;
    } else
    {
        return 0;
    }
}

figures.sort(sortall);
words.sort(sortall);

alert(figures);
alert(words);
```

Use an array to store your functions

An array is ideal to store large amounts of data like numbers, strings, and objects. A less widely known fact is that you can also store functions in an array. By calling the array element, the function will be executed. This could be used instead of the switch command. Here is an example.

```
var a=5;
var b=6;

var array_of_functions = [
    function() { c=a*b; return c },
    function() { alert('a string') },
    function() { alert('a string') },
    function() { alert('a string') }
]

d=array_of_functions[0]();
alert(d);
array_of_functions[1]();
```

alert(d) Will show 30 as the answer as the function in array_of_functions[0] is executed. Do not forget to place parentheses () at the end of the call otherwise the function will not be executed.

Using text as an array index

When an array is defined, the elements get an index number starting at 0. This gives us the elements array[0], array[1], array[2] etc. etc. Few programmers are aware that we can give the array elements a name. The next example creates an array called "languages" and uses the name of a programming language as the index. At fist every element contains the value no. Next we change the value of the element with index "javascript" to yes.

```
var languages = [];
languages["python"]="no";
languages["javascript"]="no";
languages["C++"]="o";
alert(languages["javascript"])

languages["javascript"]="yes";
```

167

```
alert(languages["javascript"])
```

We can use this array like any other array. The only problem is that we can not iterate over the array, or use array methods. The next commands will therefore not work.

```
alert("The array contains "+languages);
alert(languages.length);
alert(languages.indexOf("javascript"));
```

An array in which the elements are addressed by a name instead of an index number is called an associative array.

Using the array map method

The map function is used to alter all elements in an array with a single function. There are several ways to using map which are listed below. Use the one which is most easy/clear.

Method 1.

```
array=[1,2,3];

array=array.map(x => x * 2);
alert(array);
```

Method 2.

```
array=[1,2,3];

array = array.map(function (x) { return x * 2 })
alert(array);
```

Method 3.

```
array=[1,2,3];

function double(x) { return x * 2 }
```

```
array = array.map(double)
alert(array);
```

Method 4.

```
array=[1,2,3];

const double = x => x * 2;
array = array.map(double)
alert(array);
```

Walk through all array elements

Using the array.foreach() method, we can easily walk through an entire array.

```
var languages=["C++","Javascript","Python"];
languages.forEach
(
   function f(i)
      {
         console.log(i);
      }
)
```

Walk through an associative array

You can walk through an array by addressing the index numbers or using forEach(). However that will not work if your array is associative.

```
var learned=[]
learned["Basic"]="yes"
learned["C++"]="yes"
learned["Fortran"]="no"
learned.forEach(element => console.log(element));
```

The forEach command will not find any array elements.
To loop through an associative array you can use the next code.

```
var learned=[]
learned["Basic"]="yes"
learned["C++"]="yes"
learned["Fortran"]="no"

for (var element in learned) {
    var yesorno = learned[element];
    console.log(element, yesorno);
}
```

What is the largest number in an array

To find the largest number in an array, you could iterate through the array
with a for-loop. It is, however, shorter to use the math.max function. This
function normally does not operate on arrays, but using the spread operator
it works flawlessly.

```
var numbers = [2, 5, 3, 9, 7, 6]

maximum = Math.max(...numbers);
alert(maximum);
```

What is the second largest number in an array

To find the second largest number in an array start with finding the largest
number. Remove that number and then search again for the largest number.
Here is how to do that.

```
var array = [ 20, 15, 35, 80, 45];
var max = Math.max(...array);
array.splice(array.indexOf(max),1);
max2 = Math.max(...array);
```

```
alert(max2)
```

What is the smallest number in an array

To find the smallest number in an array you could iterate through the array with a for-loop. It is, however, shorter to use the math.min function. This function normally does not operate on arrays but using the spread operator it works flawlessly.

```
var numbers = [2, 5, 3, 9, 7, 6]

maximum = Math.min(...numbers);
alert(maximum);
```

Where to find the lowest and highest values in an array

A previous tip in this chapter shows how to find the lowest and highest numbers in an array. But where are they located.

```
var numbers = [1, 2, 1.5, 6.7];
var max = Math.max(...numbers);
var min = Math.min(...numbers);
alert(numbers.indexOf(min));
alert(numbers.indexOf(max));
```

The alerts will show respectively the place in the array where min and max are located. This only works with arrays with numbers.

Notes about arrays

Objects

Access the values of an object from within another object

We can use a value from an object as a reference to another object. In the next example there are three objects. The first object contains data about our kitchen (door open of closed and temperature) and the second object contains data about the living room (lamp on or of and temperature). The third object only contains functions that collect the data from the first two objects.

```
var kitobj =
{
    door: "closed",
    temp: "22",
};

var livingobj =
{
    lamp: "off",
    temp: "24",
};

var houseobj =
{
    getkitchen()
    {
    return "The door is "+kitobj.door + " the
temperature is " + kitobj.temp
    },
    getliving()
    {
    return "The lamp is "+livingobj.lamp + " the
temperature is " + livingobj.temp
    }
};

alert(houseobj.getkitchen());
alert(houseobj.getliving());
```

The practical use is that we can have dedicated objects for every room in our house which we only have to change when one value changes.

Add an element to an object

Adding an element to an object is simple. Just add a new key-value set.

```
var author =
  {
    name : "Luc Volders",
    languages : ["C++", "Javascript", "Lua",
"Python"]
  }
```

We can add an element to this object in two ways that both achieve the same:

```
author.booktitle = "Javascript tips"
```

or

```
author["booktitle"] = "Javascript tips"
```

Make sure, if you use the second method, to use a string as the key.

Add properties of an object to another object

The next snippet shows how to merge an objects properties into another object, without overwriting the properties and values from the first object.

```
var object01 = {key1: "C++", key2: "Javascript",
key3: "Basic"}
var object02 = {key2: "Javascript", key3: "Lua",
key4: "Python"}
function mergeobject(object01, object02)
```

```
{
    for (var key2 in object02)
    {
        if (object02.hasOwnProperty(key2) && !
object01.hasOwnProperty(key2))
        {
            object01[key2] = object02[key2];
        }
    }
    return object01;
}

alert(JSON.stringify(mergeobject(object01,object02)
))
```

This will show:
{ key1: "C++", key2: "Javascript", key3: "Basic", key4: "Python" }

The original data of key 3 is not altered and key 4 is added.

Be carefull when combining objects

It is possible to combine multiple objects into one large object. You can
achieve that with the spread operator. Just take care that all key elements
must be unique otherwise they will be overwritten. The next snippet
demonstrates this.

```
var object1 = {'a': 1, 'b': 2, 'c': 5};
var object2 = {'c': 3};
var object3 = {'d': 4};

const total = {...object1, ...object2, ...object3};

total now contains: { a: 1, b: 2, c: 3, d: 4 }
```

As you can see the value of element "c" from the first object is overwritten
by the element "c" in the second object.

Calculate the average value in an array with objects

There is a certain value in an array with objects of which we want to know the average. Start with iterating through the array and get the value out of each object and add these. Then divide that figure by the length of the array.

```
var average = 0;
var total = 0;

var temps = [
    {
        month: 'Jan',
        temp: 5
    }, {
        month: 'Feb',
        temp: 9
    }, {
        month: 'Mar',
        temp: 12
    }, {
        month: 'Apr',
        temp: 15
    }, {
        month: 'May',
        temp: 19
    }
]


for (i=0; i<temps.length; i++)
    {
    total = total + temps[i].temp;
    }
average = total / temps.length;

alert(average);
```

Convert an array to an object

The next snippet shows how to convert an array into an object.

```
var names = ['C++', 'Javascript', 'Lua', 'Python'];

var namesobj = Object.assign({}, names);

console.log(namesobj);
```

Convert an array with paired elements into an object

We have an array with strings with data pairs. The pairs are separated by a special character. The array in the example has elements like "author-Luc Volders" To convert this array into an object we can use the following method:

- Declare an empty object
- Get the length of the array
- Create a loop that goes over the length repeatedly.
- Use destructuring with the split command to separate the strings
- Put the string pairs into the object.

Here is the code that achieves that:

```
var bookarray = ["author-Luc Volders", "Title-ESP32
Simplified", "Language-English", "pages-384"];

var bookobject= {};
for (var i=0; i<bookarray.length; i++)
{
var [key, value] = bookarray[i].split("-");
bookobject [key]=value;
};

console.log(bookobject);
```

Convert an array with objects into an array

This tip shows the reverse action from the previous one. There is an array with objects, and we want it converted into an array.

```
var temperatures=
   [
        { month:"jan",temp:14},
        { month:"feb",temp:12}
   ]

var temparray = [];
for (var i = 0; i < temperatures.length; i++) {
    temparray.push((temperatures[i].month)
+":"+temperatures[i].temp);
}
alert(temparray);
```

The alert shows: jan:14, feb:12

Convert an object into an array

Using Object.values(object1) we can convert an object into an array. Here is an example.

```
var testobj =
{
  a: 'Javascript',
  b: 42,
  c: false
};

testarray=(Object.values(testobj));
alert(testarray)
```

The alert shows an array with only the values from the object.

```
testarray=(Object.keys(testobj));
alert(testarray)
```

This time the alert shows the array with the keys of the object.

```
testarray=(Object.entries(testobj));
console.log(testarray)
```

And now the alert shows the array that contains the pairs of the keys with their values. Each pair is placed in a separate subarray.

Copy an object

You can use the spread operator to copy an object like this:

```
var author = {
    name: "Luc",
    book1: "ESP32 Simplified",
    book2: "Javascript tips"
    };
var authorcopy = {...author};
console.log(authorcopy)
```

Get the highest value out of an object

If you need to distill the highest value out of an object, you can do that with the next snippet.

```
var scores =
{
    "C++": 7,
    "Javascript": 9,
    "Lua": 8,
    "Python": 8
}
```

```
function best(searchobj)
{
   var keys = Object.keys(searchobj);
   var max  = 0;
   for(var i = 0; i < keys.length; i++)
   {
      if(searchobj[keys[i]] >= max)
         {
         max = (searchobj[keys[i]]);
         };
   };
   return "Highest  = "+max;
};

alert(best(scores));
```

Get the maximum value out of an array with objects

The next snippet shows how to get the maximum value out of an array with objects using the map() function.

```
var measurements =
[
   {
     "room": "Mancave",
     "temp": 15
   },
   {
     "room": "Kitchen",
     "temp": 22
   },
    {
     "room": "Living",
     "temp": 20
   }
]
```

```
var maxtemp = Math.max(...measurements.map(m =>
m.temp))
console.log(maxtemp)
```

Get the number of keys of an object

If you need to know how many elements there are in an object, you just have to know the number of the keys. Here is how you can find that number.

```
var language = {id: 1, name: 'Javascript'}

test = Object.keys(language).length;

alert(test)
```

Get objects out of an array with objects

Using destructuring, you can get the individual objects out of an array with objects.

```
var rooms = [{name:"Kitchen"}, {name:"Mancave"},
{name:"Living"}];

var [first,second] = rooms;

console.log(first);
console.log(second.name);
```

Both variables, first and second, will contain one of the array objects.

Get relevant info out of a JSON object

A JSON object is just a Javascript object. JSON objects are often used in IOT projects to send information from a micro-controller to a computer. In this example, there is a JSON object where only information about the doors in our house is shown. The key doors contains an array that has information about the doors in our house being open or closed. The next snippet shows how to get relevant information out of the object and create a string that only shows which doors are open.

```
var alarmdoors = "";

home =
    {
    "doors":
        [{
        name: "kitchen",
        state: "open"
        },
        {
        name: "living",
        state: "open"
        },
        {
        name: "garage",
        state: "closed"
        },
        {
        name: "attick",
        state: "closed"
        }]
    }

for(var i=0; i<home.doors.length; i++)
{
   if (home.doors[i].state == "open")
     {
       alarmdoors = alarmdoors + home.doors[i].name +
" , ";
     }
```

```
}
alarmdoors = "The following doors are open " +
alarmdoors
alert (alarmdoors)
```

Get the values of an object out of an array with objects

If we need the data from an object that is part of an array with objects, we can do that with the following snippet. The snippet puts the data into a new array.

```
books =
[
{
    "Author": "Luc Volders",
    "Bookname": "ESP32 Simplified",
    "Year published": "2020",
    "Language": "english",
    "Printer": "Lulu"
},
{
    "Author": "Luc Volders",
    "Bookname": "Javascript tips",
    "Year published": "2023",
    "Language": "english",
    "Printer": "Lulu"
}
]


function bookvalues(fromarray)
{
    var keys = Object.keys(fromarray);
    var result = [];
    for(var i = 0; i < keys.length; i++)
    {
      result.push(fromarray[keys[i]]);
    };
```

```
   return result;
};
```

```
alert(bookvalues(books[1]));
```

The alert will show all the data from the second book, books[1]. That data is put in the array with the name result.

Get the values or the keys from an object out of an array

A previous tip showed how to get the values of an object out of an array. You can do this also with one line of code.

```
books =
[
{
    "Author": "Luc Volders",
    "Bookname": "ESP32 Simplified",
    "Year published": "2020",
    "Language": "english",
    "Printer": "Lulu"
},
{
    "Author": "Luc Volders",
    "Bookname": "Javascript tips",
    "Year published": "2020",
    "Language": "english",
    "Printer": "Lulu"
}
]
```

```
var result = Object.values(books[1]);
alert(result);
```

The above snippet gives you all the data from an object (book 2).

To get the keys of that object instead of the values use the next snippet:

```
var result = Object.keys(books[1]);
alert(result);
```

Get values out of an array with arrays

If you need to get a value out of an object that is filled with arrays, you can do that as follows:

```
var languages =
{
  oldlang: ["Algol", "Cobol", "Forth"],
  newlang: ["Javascript", "Lua", "Python"]
};

alert("Old language is "+languages.oldlang[1]);
alert("New language is "+languages.newlang[0]);
```

How many keys are there in an object

Here are two methods that show how many keys there are in an object.

```
var numkeys = Object.keys(myobj).length
```

The second method counts the number of keys in a for-loop:

```
var numkeys = 0;
for (let k in myobj) if (myobj.hasOwnProperty(k))
numkeys++;
```

How to change the property of a nested object

There are two ways to change the property of a nested object. The easiest is to use the dot notation. The second method is the bracket notation. Both are shown here.

Imagine a home automation system in which each room has an object with its properties.

```
var room;
var lampstate;
room = {
     "name" : "mancave",
     "temperature" : 20,
     "doorsensor" : "off",
     "lamps" : {
               "ceiling" : "on",
               "wall1" : "off"
                 }
         }
```

If we want to know if the lamp on the wall is on or off, we can retrieve that info as follows:

```
lampstate = room.lamps.wall1;
alert(lampstate);
```

With this dot notation we can also change the state of the lamp in an easy way:

```
room.lamps.wall1 = "on";
lampstate = room.lamps.wall1;
alert(lampstate);
```

To achieve this with the bracket notation use the following code:

```
lampstate = room["lamps"]["wall1"];
alert(lampstate);

room["lamps"]["wall1"] = "on";
```

```
lampstatus = room["lamps"]["wall1"];
alert(lampstate);
```

Iterate over an object

The easiest way to iterate over an object is using a for-loop. In this example
both they keys and their values are printed.

```
var object = {'a': 1, 'b': 2, 'c' : 3};

for (key in object)
{
alert(key+" : "+object[key]);
}
```

Merge multiple objects into one

It is possible to merge multiple objects into one larger object. Double
entries will be omitted. Here is an example from an IOT project in which
the information from multiple rooms is combined into one large object
representing the sensors in a house.

```
var kitchen = { lamp: "on", door: "open" };
var living = { temperature: "24", tablelamp:
"off" };
var garage = { lights: "off", gate: "closed"};
var home = Object.assign(kitchen,living,garage);
alert(JSON.stringify(home));
```

Merge multiple objects into one 2

Another method to merge multiple objects into one is by using the spread
operator. Double entries are omitted. Here is an example from an IOT

project in which the information from multiple rooms is combined into one large object representing the house.

```
var kitchen = { lamp: "on", door: "open" };
var living = { temperature: "24", tablelamp:
"off" };
var garage = { lights: "off", gate: "closed"};
var home = {...kitchen, ...living, ...garage};
alert(JSON.stringify(home));
```

Pretty print objects

Pretty print is not a widely known option in the JSON.stringify() command. Its purpose is to make objects look good. Here is an example.

```
var kitchen = { lamp: 'on', door: 'closed',
temperature: '22' };

alert(JSON.stringify(kitchen, null, 4));
```

The result looks like this:

```
{
    "lamp": "on",
    "door": "closed",
    "temperature": "22"
}
```

This only works with alert() and in the console. It will not work with document.write.

The last parameter in the command (4 in this example) determines the number of spaces used as the indent.

Remove a function from an object

Just like we can do in variables and in arrays, we can put a function in an object. If you need to remove it. first convert the object to a string with JSON.stringify() and then convert it back with JSON.parse().

```
var room = { lamp: "on", action: function()
{alert("lamp on");},
temperature: "24" };
room.action();
var room = JSON.stringify(room);
var room = JSON.parse(room);
alert(JSON.stringify(room));
```

In this example the function is executed once before it is removed.

Remove a key and value from an object

To remove a key and its value from an object, just use delete, as the next snippet demonstrates.

```
var home =
    {
    room: "attic",
    temp: 20,
    humidity: 50
    };
```

```
delete home.humidity
```

```
alert(JSON.stringify(home))
```

You can also use bracket notation like this:

```
delete home["humidity"]
```

Remove duplicates from an array with objects

Here is an example that shows how to remove duplicates from an array with objects.

```
var rooms = [
{name: "cellar"},
{name: "mancave"},
{name: "mancave"},
{name: "kitchen"},
{name: "attic"}
];

var data = Array.from(new
Set(rooms.map(JSON.stringify))).map(JSON.parse);
alert(JSON.stringify(data));
console.log(data)
```

Sort an array of objects on a key

To sort an array with objects we can use the generall sort function:

```
var sortfunc = arr => {
    arr.sort((a, b) => {
        return a-b;
    });
};
```

What we need to do is to replace a and b by the key name of the object. The next example shows how to sort an array with objects that contain information about room temperature.

```
var home = [
    {
    room: "attic",
    temp: 20
    },
```

```
      {
      room:  "garage",
      temp:   15
      },
      {
      room:  "living",
      temp:   22
      },
];

var sorttemp = arr =>
{
    arr.sort((a, b) =>
    {
        return a.temp - b.temp;
    });
};

sorttemp(home);
document.write(JSON.stringify(home));
```

Sort an array of objects on a key

Here is an example that shows how to sort an array with objects on their key.

```
var books = [
  {id: 1, name: 'ESP32 Simplified'},
  {id: 2, name: 'Raspberry Pi Pico Simplifeid'},
  {id: 3, name: 'Raspberry Pico W Simplified'},
  {id: 4, name: 'Javascript tips'}
]

function sortBooks(a, b) {
  if (a.name > b.name) {
    return 1;
  } else if (b.name > a.name) {
    return -1;
```

```
  } else {
    return 0;
  }
}

books.sort(sortBooks);

console.log(books)
```

Store objects in localstorage

You can only store strings in localstorage. If you need to store an object, first convert it into a string, like this:

```
var myobject = { 'one': 1, 'two': 2, 'three': 3 };
localStorage.setItem('myobject',
JSON.stringify(myobject));
```

To retrieve the object use:

```
var myobject = localStorage.getItem('myobject');
myobject=JSON.parse(myobject)
```

to show the object use:

```
alert('myobject: '+ JSON.stringify(myobject));
```

Test if a key exists

In an IOT project, you might have an object, in which temperature values are stored. When you need to know if the temperature you want to check already has been registered. This is how you can check that.

```
var temperature={"kitchen":20,"living":22}
```

```
var kitavail =
temperature.hasOwnProperty("kitchen");
var manavail=
temperature.hasOwnProperty("mancave");
alert(kitavail)
alert(manavail)
```

Test if an element exists in an array with objects

To check if an element exists in an array with objects, you can use the next snippet.

```
var array = [
  { id: 1, room: 'Mancave' },
  { id: 2, room: 'Kitchen'},
  { id: 3, room: 'Cellar' }];

function roomexists(room) {
  return array.some(function(el) {
    return el.room === room;
  });
}

console.log(roomexists('Kitchen'));
console.log(roomexists('Attick'));
```

Test if an object is empty

It is easy to test if an object is empty. Just test if the length of the keys is zero. Here is an example that demonstrates this.

```
var language = {id: 1, name: 'Javascript'}

test = Object.keys(language).length === 0;
alert(test)
```

Test whether two objects are fully identical

We can not use == or === to compare two objects. To compare them, first convert them to a string. The following example shows how this is done.

```
var obj1 = {Room: "mancave", sensor: 'lamp',
status: "on" };
var obj2 = {Room: "mancave", sensor: 'lamp',
status: "on" };

alert(JSON.stringify(obj1) ===
JSON.stringify(obj2));
```

The slightest variation like a capital letter, or a mix up of the elements, makes the alert show "false".

Notes about objects

Functions

A function in a variable

We can put a function into a variable. This can be done with anonymous functions and with named functions.

The next lines show an alert() which calls a variable that does not have a value but calls an anonymous function.

```
var test = function()
{
return "anonymous function executed";
}

alert(test());
```

The next lines perform the same action but here the function is a named function:

```
var testfunc = function test()
{
return "The function test is executed";
}

alert(testfunc());
```

The function test() is enclosed in the variable and can not be called separately.

Call a function with a condition

Generally, a function is called with a variable. It is also possible to call a function with a condition. Here is an example.

```
function test (tryme)
{
alert(tryme)
}
```

```
test(3>6)
```

The function test is called with (3>6). As this is false the alert will show "false"

```
test(3*16)
```

In this example the outcome is first calculated and then sent to the function. The alert therefore will show 18.

Call a function with an unknown number of arguments

Normally when we call a function we know how many arguments we pass.

For example:

```
var a=1, b="hello", c=3, d="world"
function(a, b, c, d)
```

If we need to call a function from several places in our script, we may not know upfront how many arguments we are going to pass. The solution is to have the function itself examine how many arguments are passed:

```
function unknownnumber(a)
{
    alert("first argument: " + a);
    alert("number of arguments passed: " +
arguments.length);
    alert(arguments[3]);
}

var a=1, b="hello", c=3, d="world";
unknownnumber(a,b,c,d)
```

Arguments are passed to a function in some kind of array. Using arguments.length we can examine how many arguments were passed and the arguments can be used just like an array value using arguments[index].

Call a function with an unknown number of arguments 2

The previous tip showed a method to call a function with an unknown number of parameters. There is another method. You can use the spread operator.

```
function testfunction(...parameters)
{
    alert(parameters);
}

testfunction(1, 2, 3, 4);
```

To iterate through the parameters you can use the next snippet.

```
function testfunction(...parameters)
{
    for(var value of parameters)
    {
        alert(value);
    }
}

testfunction(1, 2, 3, 4, 5);
```

Call a function with default arguments

When calling a function it expects a certain number of arguments. When calling the function with to few arguments you can get faulty results. The next snippet shows how to predefine default values in a function which can be overruled during the function call.

```
function welcome(name, text="Hello ")
{
return text + name;
}
```

```
alert(welcome("Luc");
alert(welcome("Luc", "Good to see you "));
```

The first alert uses the name and the default value, and returns: Hello Luc
The second alert uses both parameters, and returns: Good to see you Luc

This works with calculations too:

```
function calculate(amount, times=2)
{
return amount * times;
}

alert(calculate(3));
alert(calculate(3,4));
```

The first alert uses the amount and the default value for times (2) which results in 6.
The second alert uses both parameters and therefore returns 12.

Convert a string into a function

A function can be build from a string using the following method:

```
var myfunc = new Function (string)
```

Here is an example that demonstrates this.

```
var string = "alert('Hello World');"

var myfunc =new Function (string);

myfunc()
```

Be careful with this. It is tempting to have an html input field in which someone can type a function and then execute this. This poses however a sincere security risk.

How to bypass a default parameter

A previous tip discussed how to use a function with default arguments. Here is how you can bypass one of the default arguments.

```
function myfunc(x, y=15, z=3)
{
  console.log(x*y);
  console.log(z);
}

myfunc(2,undefined,22)
```

In this example the console will show:
30
22

As the function is called with "undefined" as the second parameter, that part of the function is executed with the default parameter.

Repeat a function regularly

With setInterval(function, milliseconds) you can repeat a function at regular intervals. The most efficient thing to do is to put the function call in a variable. That way, you can disable it with clearInterval. The next example activates a function every 5 seconds and places an alert on your screen. The setTimeout() instruction disables the interval after 25 seconds.

```
<!DOCTYPE html>
<html>
<title>Repeat a function regularly</title>
<head>
<script>
var repeat = setInterval(often, 5000 );
var stoprepeat = setTimeout(stop, 25000);

function often()
{
```

```
alert("5 secs");
}

function stop()
{
clearInterval(repeat);
}

</script>
</head>
<body>
</body>
</html>
```

Repeat a function regularly but a pre-defined number of times

You can execute a function every x seconds or minutes. But what if you want to do that a predefined number of times. The next snippet shows how to do that.

```
for(var i = 0; i < 5; i++)
{
    (function(xtimes)
        {
        setTimeout(function()
          {
          alert(xtimes);
          }, xtimes*5000);
        })(i);
}
```

The for loop decides how many times the function will get executedm: in this example 5 times. The number 5000 tells the function to repeat every 5 seconds.

Stop a function in an interval

Generally, a function performs a task and then stops. There are, however, also functions that constant perform a certain task in the background. How to stop such a function is what we are going to show here. A previous tip (Repeat a function regularly) showed how to stop a function after a certain time. Use setInterval for this and stop the function with clearInterval. This can be done at a certain time interval, but we can also do this by pushing a button.

HTML part:

```
<button type="button" onclick =
"start()">Start</button>
<button type="button" onclick =
"stop()">Stop</button>
<p id="testid">======</p>
```

Javascript part:

```
<script>
var timefunction = null;
var i=0;
function start()
{
    timefunction = setInterval(function()
    {
        i=i+1

document.getElementById("testid").innerHTML=i;
    }, 1000);
}

function stop()
{
    alert("The function is stopped")
    clearInterval(timefunction);
}
</script>
```

In this example the function increases a number every second and puts it into a <p> tag. This is repeated until we press the"Stop" button.

Test if an argument is passed to a function

If a function should be called with multiple arguments and only one argument is given, the function might raise an error if any action is taken on the missing argument. The next snippet shows how you can test if an argument is passed.

```
function func(arg1, arg2) {
  if (typeof arg2 === "undefined") {
     arg2 = "second arg not available";
  }

  alert(arg1+ " , "+ arg2)
}

func("Mancave")
```

Warning if a parameter is forgotten in a function call

This tip gives some extra functionality to the earlier tip with the name: Call a function with default arguments. That tip shows how to pass a default value to a function when a parameter is omitted.

Instead of passing a standard value you can also pass a function. This allows to give a warning if a parameter is omitted. Here is an example.

```
function fault()
{
alert("Hey, fill it in !!");
return "Nobody";
};
```

```
function welcome(name = fault(), text="Hello ")
{
return text + name;
}

alert(welcome());
alert(welcome("Luc", "Good to see you "));
```

If you call the function without the name the alert will show "Hey, fill it in !!" and the value "Nobody" is passed to the original function. You should take some action on that. It is possible to test for a faulty name in the original function (welcome), but using an extra function can keep things well organized.

Notes about functions

Communication

CSV to array

When you receive a file from an external server it can be in the CSV format (comma separated values). To work with the data in such a file it is the easiest to put the data into an array. This is how you can do that:

```
var csvstring = "arduino, ESP8266, ESP32, Microbit,
Raspberry";

var array = csvstring.split(",");
alert(array);
```

Encode a string for sending data

In many cases when we want to send data, over the Internet, to another computer or server, it is necessary to replace the spaces in a text by the code %20
If we want, for example, to send the following text: "the temperature is 15 degrees" we need to encode it as follows: "the%20temperature%20is%2015%20degrees"
We can achieve this easily with the following lines of code:

```
var normal = "the temperature is 15 degrees";
var coded = encodeURI(normal);
```

Decode a received string

When we receive data from a server or other computer often the spaces in the text are replaced by the code %20. Apparently the Internet does not like spaces. So if we receive a text like: the temperature is 15 degrees it will be received as follows: the%20temperature%20is%2015%20degrees This can be easily converted to the original form with the next lines of code:

```
var coded = "the%20temperature%20is
%2015%20degrees";
var normal = decodeURI(coded);

alert(normal);
```

Mask an email address

Sometimes you want to mask an e-mail address on a webpage. You can do that with the next snippet.

```
var email = "myname@company.com";

var [name, provider] = email.split('@');
var helpname = name[0] + '...' + name[name.length
-1];
var hidden = helpname + '@' + provider;

console.log(hidden);
```

In this example the console will show: m...e@company.com

What is my ip address

If you need to know the users ip address you can use the next snippet

```
fetch('https://api.ipify.org/?format=json').
    then(results => results.json()).
    then(data => console.log(data.ip))
```

Notes about communication

216

Various

Alert, confirm and prompt

Using alert allows to present text, or data, in a pop-up window. This is often used in this book like this:

```
alert("this is an alarm")
```

There is also a less known option to get a confirmation from a user. It works like this:

```
if (confirm("Are you sure"))
   {
   alert( "Ok you are certain");
   }
else
   {
   alert( "You are still in doubt");
   }
```

And even less widely known is, that we can ask the user for information in a pop-up window, like this:

```
var answer = (prompt('please enter a number'))
```

```
alert(answer)
```

Please be aware that the answer is always a string even if you entered a number.

And can have weird outcomes

The AND function is used to test conditions and gives a boolean value as outcome:

```
var first = 3;
var second = 6;
```

```
alert(first < 4 && second > 4);
```

The alert will show "true" as both comparisons are true.

However using the AND function, when the comparisons do not give a boolean value, will show the last value:

```
alert(first < 4 && second > 4 && 6 && 90);
```

The alert will now show 90.

```
alert("today" && "tomorrow");
```

Now the alert will show "tomorrow".

Another way to write one-line comments

Normally a one-line comment is written like this:

```
// this is a comment
```

But this is also valid:

```
<!-- this is also a comment.
```

Officially, this is a html comment, but Javascript accepts it too.

Array with functions instead of switch

It is perfectly possible to replace a switch command with an array with functions. This is faster and often shorter to program. The disadvantage is that this only works when the parameter is a number.

This is a normal switch setup:

```
var number = 1;
switch(number)
    {
    case 1:
        alert("number 1");
        break;
    case 2:
        alert("number 2");
        break;
    case 3:
        alert("number 3");
        break;
    }
```

We can replace this with:

```
var number = 1;

testarray =
    [
    function(){alert("number 1")},
    function(){alert("number 2")},
    function(){alert("number 3")}
    ];

testarray[number]();
```

Ask for a color and count the number of times it is chosen

This program checks for a color. You can enter red or blue which are not case sensitive. Every time you enter the right name of the color the value in the object is increased. By pressing cancel you will get the total amounts.

```
var items =
{
    red: 0,
    blue: 0
```

```
    };

function getitems()
{
  while(true)
  {
    var itemtype = prompt('Enter RED or BLUE for
adding items, cancel to quit');
    if(itemtype === null) break;
    switch(itemtype.toLowerCase())
    {
      case "red": items.red++; break;
      case "blue": items.blue++; break;
      default: alert("Please enter RED or BLUE");
    }
  }
  alert(`Red : ${items.red}, Blue : $
{items.blue}`);
};
getitems()
```

Assign a default value to a variable

A variable may exist but may not have gotten a value assigned, and
therefore might be empty. Using that variable in your program may give
unpredictable results, or throw an error and crash the program. The solution
is to give the variable a default value which can be done as follows:

```
var author = "Luc ";
var country ;
country = country || "The Netherlands";
alert(author + country);
```

The || comparison returns the second value if the first value is empty.

This works slightly different when used with objects:

```
var origin =
```

223

```
{
name: 'Luc',
country: null
};
var country = origin.country || "The Netherlands";
alert(origin.name + " " + country);
```

The default value "The Netherlands" will be shown if the country element in the object has the value: "", 0, null or undefined.

Clear all intervals

To stop all intervals in your script, you can use this snippet.

```
var interval_id = window.setInterval(()=>{},
99999);

for (var i = 0; i < interval_id; i++)
    window.clearInterval(i);
```

Clear local storage

There are two ways to clear Local Storage. The first method is by using clear().

```
localStorage.clear();
```

The second method is by iterating over all elements and deleting the keys.

```
for(key in localStorage)
{
delete localStorage[key];
}
```

Convert a boolean value to a string

A Boolean variable holds the value true or false. If you need to convert the value into a string you can do that with variable.toString like this :

```
bool = true
alert(typeof(bool))

stringbool = bool.toString()
alert(typeof(stringbool))
```

Convert a variable name to a string

The next tip shows how you can convert the name of a variable into a string.

```
var name = 'John'
varname = Object.keys({name})[0]
alert(varname)
```

Convert a variable to a boolean value

If you need to convert a variable into a Boolean (true or false) value you can do that with the double negate (!!) function. You can use this for example in a while loop.

```
var a = ""
!a gives true
!!a  gives false

var a = "hallo"
!a gives false
!!a gives true

var a = 0
!a gives true
!!a gives false
```

Convert a RGB value into hexadecimal

The next snippet converts an RGB value into a hex value. You can use this to set the color of an element on your webpage,

```
function rgbintohex (r, g, b)
{
return   "#" + ((1 << 24) + (r << 16) + (g << 8) +
b).toString(16).slice(1);
}

var hex = rgbintohex(255, 51, 255);
alert(hex)
```

Convert ASCII codes into a string

When working with sensors in an IOT project, they might send their data as ASCII codes instead of strings. The next line shows how to convert the ASCII codes into strings.

```
String.fromCharCode(65,66,67);
```

Delay in a foreach loop

If you want to put a delay into a foreach loop, you can use the following example.

```
var numbers=[1,2,3,4,5]
var i=0

numbers.forEach((element,i) => {
    setTimeout(function()
        {
         alert(element), i * 2000);
        });
```

226

In this example, the array elements are every 2 seconds shown in an alert.

Delay in a loop

If you need to delay while iterating here is how its done.

```
var counter = 1;
var times = 10;

function testloop()
{
  setTimeout(function()
    {
    console.log('Javascript Tips '+ counter);
    counter++;
    if (counter < times)
    {
       testloop();
    }
  }, 3000)
}

testloop();
```

Each time after counter is incremented, we test if the value is lower then times, and if so we call the function again.

Determine screen width and height

To get the screen resolution width and height, you can use the next snippet.

```
alert("The screenwidth is: "+screen.width);
alert("The screenheightis: "+screen.height);
```

Encrypt and decode (base 64)

The commands btoa and atob allow for encrypting text and numbers in an easy way. Here is an example:

```
var text = 'Javascript tips';

var encoded = window.btoa(text);
alert(encoded);

var decoded = window.atob(encoded);
alert(decoded)
```

Escape characters

Here is a list of the most common escape characters used to format text.

```
\'  — Single quote
\"  — Double quote
\\  — Backslash
\b  — Backspace
\f  — Form feed
\n  — New line
\r  — Carriage return
\t  — Horizontal tabulator
\v  — Vertical tabulator
```

Evaluate a string

The command eval() ables you to run a command, or a function, that is input by the user, or fetched from another page.
Here is an example.

```
string = eval(new String('2 + 2'))
```

This creates a new string with the name string, and the content "2 + 2"

```
answer = eval (2 + 2)
```

In this example the variable answer gets the value 4.

Forget OR use switch-case

It is obvious that using switch-case in stead of multiple if statements is much more organized and clear. Much less known is that it is also much clearer to use switch-case in stead of an if statement with multiple OR tests. The next example demonstrates this.

```
var language = "Javascript";

if (language == 'Javascript' || language == 'C++'
|| language == 'Python' )
   { console.log('The most frequently used
programming languages')
   }

switch (language)
{
   case 'Javascript':
   case 'C++':
   case 'Python':
   console.log('The most frequently used programming
languages')
}
```

Both statements do the same, but the switch-case statements look more organized, and are easier to debug.

Generate a password of x characters

If you want to generate a password of x characters, use the following snippet.

```
function newpass(numberchars)
{
  var password = "";
  var letters =
"ABCDEFGHIJKLMNOPQRSTUVWXYZabcdefghijklmnopqrstuvwx
yz0123456789";
  for (var i = 0; i < numberchars; i++)
  {
    password +=
letters.charAt(Math.round(Math.random() *
letters.length));
  }
  return password;
}

alert(newpass(10));
```

Generate a password of x characters 2

The next code shows how to generate a password of x characters.
The number of letters in the password is put in the variable amount. Next we generate a random number from 1 to 26 and add that to 97. 97 is the first number for the ASCII code for letters in the alphabet.

```
var amount = 8;
function password(amount)
{
    var newpas = '';
    for(var i = 0; i < amount; i++)
    {
        var rand = Math.floor(Math.random() * 27);
        newpas += String.fromCharCode(97 + rand);
```

```
    };
    return newpas;
};
newpassword = password(8)
alert(newpassword);
```

Generate a pseudo random number

You can generate a large pseudo random number, by taking the time or part of it. Here is an example.

```
newrand = Number(new Date())
alert (newrand)
```

Generate a random hex value

The next snippet shows how to generate a random hex value.

```
var hex =
Math.floor(Math.random()*16777215).toString(16);
var hex = "#" + hex
alert(hex)
```

Get a random hex color

If you need a random hex color code you can generate it with the following snippet.

```
var hexletters = '0123456789ABCDEF';
var color = '';
while(color.length < 6)
   {
        var random = Math.floor(Math.random() * 16);
```

```
        color += hexletters[random];
    };
color = "#" + color;
alert(color);
```

Get a random number within a certain range

To get a random number, that falls within a certain range, you can use the following snippet:

```
var minimum = 100;
var maximum = 200;
var difference = maximum-minimum;
var randomval = Math.random();

var newnumber = Math.floor((randomval * difference)
+ minimum);

alert(newnumber);
```

Get a list of all variables in a page

The next snippet shows how to obtain a list of all variables that are used in the current webpage.

```
var variables = "";
for (var name in this) variables += name + "\n";
alert(variables);
```

Give multiple variables simultaneous the same value

If you want to give multiple variables the same value simultaneous you can use the following code.

```
var i;
var j;
var k;
var count;
var begin;

var i=j=k=count=begin=1;
```

You can use this also with strings.

Inspect what is stored in localstorage

You can find what is stored in localstorage with the following program lines.

```
var i;

console.log("local storage");
for (i = 0; i < localStorage.length; i++)
   {
   console.log(localStorage.key(i) + "=[" +
localStorage.getItem(localStorage.key(i)) + "]");
   }
```

Inspect what is stored in sessionstorage

Using the next lines you can find what is stored in session storage.

```
console.log("session storage");
for (i = 0; i < sessionStorage.length; i++)
   {
   console.log(sessionStorage.key(i) + "=[" +
sessionStorage.getItem(sessionStorage.key(i)) +
"]");
   }
```

Localstorage only stores strings

Maybe obvious but I had to mention it anyway.
You can only store strings in Localstorage.

Localstorage can pose a safety problem

Local storage can be used to temporarily store data. This can pose a safety breech, as the data is stored on your local harddisk, and is not encrypted or password protected. Other programs or Javascript scripts can get access to that data and even alter it. So be careful with what you store in localstorage.

Make your code looking good

If your program is (finally) ready, you need to document it for future use. One of the things that makes code easier to read is to have indents, brackets etc. consistent all over the code. The next website allows you to paste your code and makes it looking good.

https://beautifier.io/

Make your code run endlessly

The following trick makes your code run endlessly.

```
var a=0;
while(true)
   {
      alert(a++)
   }
```

While true is, of course, always true, this loop will run endless

Measure how long a function or part of code runs

You might want to know how long it takes for a function, or a block of code, to run. Testing the performance might show the need to optimize for speed. In this book there is a tip that tells how to pause a program. We use that here and measure how long the pause took.

```
var startTime = performance.now();

// pause 2000 millieseconds
var millies = 2000;
var start = new Date().getTime();
var end = start;
while(end < start + millies)
{
  end = new Date().getTime();
}

var endTime = performance.now();
var totalTime=endTime-startTime;

alert('Total time:'+totalTime +'ms');
```

Measure the performance of a code block

During developing software you might wonder how fast the code you are writing is. You can measure this with console.time and console.timeEnd. The time measured is only shown in the console (hence the name). Here is an example.

```
console.time("primeornot");
function testprime()
{
  if (figure===1)
  {
    return false;
  }
```

```
  if(figure === 2)
  {
    return true;
  }
  if (figure > 2)
  {
    for(var x = 2; x < figure; x++)
    {
      if(figure % x === 0)
      {
        return false;
      }
    }
    return true;
  }
}
console.log(testprime(155035219));

console.timeEnd("primeornot");
```

Multiple lines in an alert

When showing an alert, most of the time, all information is shown on a single line. You can make things more clear, by showing the information on multiple lines. To get multiple lines use \r\n in your text, like the next snippet demonstrates.

```
var text = "Javascript Tips \r\n";
text = text + "Luc Volders \r\n";
text = text + "English version"
alert(text);
```

Pause in Javascript

If you need a pause (sleep, delay) function in your program, you can use the next snippet.

```
function pause(ms)
{
    var time = new Date();
    var time2 = null;
    do { time2 = new Date(); }
    while(time2-time < ms);
}

pause(5000)
alert("5 seconds later")
```

Pause in Javascript 2

To pause your script you can use the next snippet. The variable millies contains the time in milliseconds.

```
var millies = 2000;
var start = new Date().getTime();
var end = start;
while(end < start + millies) {
   end = new Date().getTime();
}
alert("time is up")
```

Press a single key to activate a function

The next code shows how you can intercept a key press, to activate a function. Pressing the letter d on your keyboard makes the background color of the page black. Pressing the letter l sets it back to default.

```
document.addEventListener('keydown', function
(event)
  {
  if (event.key === 'd')
    {
    document.body.style = "color: white;
background-color: black";
    }
  if (event.key === 'l')
    {
    document.body.style = '';
    }
  });
```

Press CTRL or ALT and a key to activate a function

In the previous tip you saw how to intercept a key-press. But sometimes you want not to just intercept a key, but a CTRL-key combination. To achieve that the code is almost the same.

```
document.addEventListener('keydown', function
(event) {
  // CTRL + d makes background dark
  if (event.ctrlKey && event.key === 'd') {
    document.body.style = "color: white;
background-color: #111111";
  }
  // CTRL + l sets background back to original
  if (event.ctrlKey && event.key === 'l') {
    document.body.style = '';
  }
});
```

If you want to catch the ALT key just replace ctrlKey by altKey

Press CTRL or ALT and a key to activate4 a function 2

The previous tip showed how to intercept the CTRL-key or ALT-key to perform your own function. However, certain combinations have pre-defined functions. CTRL-d in Windows for example is meant to add a bookmark. In the previous example, therefore, the bookmark screen was opened AND the background color changed. To prevent activating the Windows standard functions add event.preventDefault() like the following snippet demonstrates.

```
document.addEventListener('keydown', function
(event) {
  event.preventDefault()
  // CTRL + d makes background dark
  if (event.ctrlKey && event.key === 'd') {
    document.body.style = "color: white;
background-color: #111111";
  }
  // CTRL + 1 sets background back to original
  if (event.ctrlKey && event.key === 'l') {
    document.body.style = '';
  }
});
```


Prevent errors

Here is a simple method to prevent errors in formula's or commands.

```
var a = "";
alert(a*a || 0);
```

Using || 0 will become 0 if the formula throws an error. Here are some more examples.

```
alert(0/0 || 0);
alert(" "*5 || 0);
```

You can also replace the 0 by an error message, like the following shows:

```
alert(0/0 || "error !!");
```

Prevent printing part of the page

Using CSS code, you can prevent part of a page being printed. The part will be visible on the computer screen, but will not be printed on paper. The next example shows how to do that.

```
<html>
<style>
@media print
{
#non-printable { display: none; }
#printable { display: block; }
}
</style>

<body>

<div id="non-printable"  style = "color:red">
This is the first line of a text that will not be
printed<br>
And this line will also not be printed<br>
</div>

<div id="printable" style = "color:green">
This is the first line that will be printed.<br>
And this line will also get on paper.
</div>

</body>
</html>
```

In this example, there are two DIV's, which both can be seen on your screen, but the text from the first DIV can not be printed. Using display:none allows us to hide part of a page. As we have attached that to @media print this part will be hidden on your printer.

Random true or false

If you need a random true or false value (like head or tails in a game) you can check if Math.random() is larger then 0.5 as the next snippet shows.

```
function randbool()
{
return Math.random() >= 0.5;
}

alert(randbool());
```

Remove a variable from localstorage

Variables can be stored in localstorage for later use. And sometimes you will want to remove a variable from localstorage. You can do that with:

```
window.localStorage.removeItem("my_item_key");
```

Skip a step in a loop

In a loop, you can test the condition of a variable, and act on it. You can also test for a variable, and skip the next code using the command continue; Here is an example.

```
for (var i = 1; i<10; i++)
{
   if (i ==5)
     {continue}
   console.log(i)
}
```

Every number from 1 to 10 will be printed in the console except 5.

Speak out your texts

Every web browser has a build in speech synthesizer. This means that you can have all the texts on your webpage, or variables, spoken out loud. Making the webpage speak is easy. Just use:

```
speechSynthesis.speak(new
SpeechSynthesisUtterance('Hello World'));
```

By altering some parameters you can influence the language and speed in which the sentences are spoken.

```
var u = new SpeechSynthesisUtterance();
u.text = 'This is really good English';
u.lang = 'en-US';
u.rate = 1.2;
speechSynthesis.speak(u);
```

The voice is browser dependent. So the spoken words sound different when the webpage is shown on Firefox or Chrome. But the pronunciation is generally excellent.

For other languages, you can use the letter codes from the BCP 47 language tag, like:

```
English, United States : en-US
German, Germany : de-DE
Spanish : es-ES_tradnl
French, France : fr-FR
Japanese, Japan : ja-JP
Portuguese, Brazil : pt-BR
Russian, Russian Federation : ru-RU
Hindi, India : hi-IN
Chinese, China : zh-CN
English, United Kingdom : en-GB */
```

Stop a loop after some time

Some loops run indefinitely. The next code shows how you can stop such a loop, after a predefined period of time.

```
var looprunning = true;
var i=0;

setTimeout(function () {
  looprunning = false;
}, 100);

while ( looprunning ) {
  i++
  console.log(i)
```

Stop running code on a condition

We can put code into a block and stop running that code if a certain condition is met. The next snippet shows how to do this.

```
var stopcondition = 5;

testblock:
  {
  alert('This text is shown');
  if (stopcondition == 5)
     {
  break testblock;
     }
  alert('This line is not shown');
  }
alert("here continues the rest of the code");
```

Store large amounts of data

A program can temporarily store a large amount of data in localstorage by converting the data into array. Here is an example.

```
myarray = [1,"Luc",2,3,"newbook"]
localStorage.setItem("mytest",
JSON.stringify(myarray))
```

Keep in mind that all items need to be converted into a string.

To retrieve the data you can use the next code:

```
arraytwo =
JSON.parse(localStorage.getItem("mytest"))
```

You can get the individual items back by adressing the array elements:

```
alert(JSON.stringify(arraytwo[0]))
```

Store data in a file

Javascript is very cautious about doing things on your harddisk. Nevertheless, there is a way to store the collected data in a file on your computer. Put the data in the variable testtext, and the data will be downloaded as a file to your computer with the filename example.txt

```
<!DOCTYPE html>
<html>
<script>
window.onload = function(){
function download(filename, text) {
  var element = document.createElement('a');
  element.setAttribute('href',
'data:text/plain;charset=utf-8,' +
encodeURIComponent(text));
  element.setAttribute('download', filename);
```

```javascript
    element.style.display = 'none';
    document.body.appendChild(element);

    element.click();

    document.body.removeChild(element);
}

// Start file download.

var testtext = "Hello world. This is a test.\nThis
starts on a new line.\nAnd here is another line";
download("example.txt", testtext);
alert("done")
}
</script>
</html>
```

You need to put this into the window.onload = function(){} otherwise it will not execute.

Switch case with comparisons

Swtch-case is ideal for testing a bunch of variables. It is however only possible to test absolute values.

```javascript
var temperature = 18;

switch(temperature)
  {
  case 15:
    alert("Cold");
    break;
  case 20:
    alert ("Just right");
    break;
  default:
    alert("Not in test sequence");
```

```
}
```

In this situation "Not in test sequence" is shown.
It would be more convenient, if we could do tests like larger than (>) or smaller than (<). This is possible with the trick shown in the next snippet.

```
function gettemperature(temp)
    {
    var feelslike = "";
    switch (true)
        {
        case isNaN(temp):
            feelslike = "No figure given";
            break;
        case (temp >= 25):
            feelslike = "Hot";
            break;
        case (temp <= 18):
            feelslike = "Cold";
            break;
        default:
            feelslike = "Normal";
            break;
        };
    return feelslike;
    }
alert(gettemperature(20));
```

By putting switch inside a function. it is possible to use comparisons.

Switch case with multiple parameters

Normally, switch-case is used with a single parameter in each case statement. It is not widely known that you can put multiple parameters in the case statement. Here is an example that shows how to do this.

```
var room = "bedroom";
var upordown="";
```

```
switch(room) {
    case "cellar":case "kitchen":case "mancave":
        upordown = "Downstairs";
        break;
    case "bedroom":case "shower":case "attic":
        upordown = "Upstairs";
        break;
    default:
        upordown = "Unknown";
}
alert(upordown)
```

Cellar, kitchen, and mancave will all give Downstairs as an answer. Bedroom, shower, and attic will each give Upstairs as the answer.

Switch case with return statements

By placing a switch-case statement inside a function, we can place the outcome of the test in a return statement, just like in a normal function. The next snippet shows how to achieve this.

```
function gettemperature(temp)
    {
    var tempfeel = "";
    switch (true)
        {
        case isNaN(temp):
            return "No figure given";
            break;
        case (temp >= 25):
            tempfeel = "Hot";
            return tempfeel;
            break;
        case (temp <= 18):
            tempfeel = "Cold";
            return tempfeel;
            break;
        default:
```

```
          tempfeel = "normal";
          return tempfeel;
      break;
    };
  }
alert(gettemperature("20"));
```

Switch-Case

If we need to choose between many options, the switch-case commands are more efficient than using a lot of if-thens. A drawback is that when working with strings, this is case-sensitive. The words need to match exactly. If case needs to react on "Javascript" then "javascript" will not activate the case function. To avoid these kinds of problems, convert the search-string to lowercase (or uppercase) as the next example shows.

```
var teststring = "Javascript";
teststring = teststring.toLowerCase();
switch (teststring)
  {
  case 'javascript':
    alert("Javascript chosen");
    break;
  case 'python':
    alert("To bad you chose Python");
    break;
  default:
    alert("Totally wrong")
  }
```

Swap two or more variables

Here is a fast method that shows how to swap the contents of several variables.

```
var a = 100;
var b = 10;
var c = 5;
[a, b, c] = [c, a, b];
```

a will get the value of c, b will get the value of a, and c will get the value of b.

Test if a variable exists

In the HTML section, you can find a snippet that shows all the variables that are used on a page. If you just need to know if a certain variable exists, you can use the next snippet. In this example, we test if the variable test3345 exists.

```
if (typeof(test3345) !== undefined) {
    alert("unknown varaiable")
}
```

Test if a variable is empty

A variable might be declared, but not yet given a value. When you perform an operation on that variable, you might get an error. The next snippet shows how you can test if a variable is empty, to prevent these errors.

```
var test;

if (Boolean(test))
   {
     alert ("variabele has a value");
   }
else
   {
     alert ("variabele is empty");
   }
```

Test if the browser supports touch events

Sometimes, you need to know if a program runs on a computer, tablet, or phone. You can test that by checking if the touch events are supported, as the following code shows:

```
var touchscreen = () =>
  window && 'ontouchstart' in window;

alert(touchscreen());
```

Test if localstorage is activated

We can use localstorage for storing data that can be used later on. This might pose a problem if the user, or one of his programs, has disabled localstorage. The next snippet shows how to test whether localstorage is activated or not.

```
function localtest ()
{
  try
  {
    var item = "tipstest";
    var value = "yes or no";
    localStorage.setItem(item, value);
    localStorage.removeItem(item);
    return true;
  }
  catch (e)
  {
    return false;
  }
};

alert(localtest());
```

Test if localstorage is used or empty

To test if localstorage contains elements or not, you can use the next snippet.

```
if (localStorage.length > 0)
   {
     alert("There are elements in localstorage")
   }
else
   {
     alert("Local storage is empty")
   }
```

Test if sessionstorage is activated

Sessionstorage can be used if you need to store information while the current window is open. However, it's possible that the user or one of his programs has turned off session storage. Use the following snippet to determine whether session storage is enabled.

```
function sessiontest ()
{
   try
   {
     var item = "tipstest";
     var value = "yes or no";
     sessionStorage.setItem(item, value);
     sessionStorage.removeItem(item);
     return true;
   }
   catch (e)
   {
     return false;
   }
};

alert(sessiontest());
```

Test if the user is on line

There are several reasons why you should check if a user is online.
If the user is not online you can, for example, not use external
storage or libraries. To test whether the user is online use the next snippet.

```
if (navigator.onLine==true)
{
alert("user is on line");
}
```

Toggle a boolean variable

Here is a really easy way to toggle a Boolean variable. Toggling means that
True becomes False and the other way round. It is done with the !(not)
operator.

```
thing = True
thing = !thing
```

Use AND as a replacement for if()

It is possible to use && as a replacement for an if() command. This only
works on a single line.

```
var test = 10;
test == 10 &&  alert ("Yes")
```

This is the same as if (test = 10) {alert ("Yes")}

The difference with an if() construction is that if() can use multiple lines,
with && everything must be on the same line.

Use OR to give a variable a default value

We can use || to give a variable a default value.

```
var test = 0;
test = test || 10;
alert(test)
```

In this example, test will get the value 10.
Actually, this is the same as.

```
if (test = 0) {test = 10};
```

This works if test = 0 but also if test = "" or undefined or false.

Use OR to test if a variable is falsey

We can use the previous tip in another way to test if a variable is falsey and act on that.

```
Vat test = 0;
test = test || alert("empty")
```

Replace the alert by a function or any other Javascript command you need

Use prompt for a quick answer

We can use prompts to get a quick answer from a user. This snippet shows how to test what the user entered.

```
var name = prompt("What is your name");
if (name === "")
{
   alert("Please, fill in your name");
}
```

253

```
else
{
  alert("Hello : " + name);
}
```

What is syntactic sugar (software candy)

Syntactic sugar means that the new features of the language are not really new. Instead, they are a different syntax for something that already exists. You could do exactly the same by writing something in a different way in the old version.

An example is the arrow function. You can use the arrow functions or the old equivalent. The arrow functions do not offer anything new. Other examples are the ternary operator, which is just a substitution for if – else and the AT parameter for pointing to an array index.

Where is the mouse on your screen

The next lines of code display the mouse location every second in the console window.

```
<!DOCTYPE html>
<html>
<title>Online Javascript Editor</title>
<head>
<script>
var horizontal = -1;
var vertical = -1;
document.onmousemove = function(event) {
      horizontal = event.pageX;
      vertical = event.pageY;
}
setInterval(mouselocation, 1000);
```

```
function mouselocation() {
      console.log('Cursor at: '+horizontal+',
'+vertical);
}
</script>
</head>
<body>
```

Where is this webpage hosted

It might be necessary to know where the current webpage is coming from. It might be a stored on a remote server or as a local file. Think about safety: we need to make sure that the page is loaded from the right server or from the right subdirectory.

We can get the current location of the webpage with the following commands:

```
var protocol = window.location.protocol;
var server = window.location.host;
var path = window.location.pathname;
```

protocol will be file: or http: or https:
server will provide the name of the server or nothing
path provides the name of the subdirectory

Where is this webpage hosted 2

Here is another way to find the location from which the current webpage is loaded. This way, you can see if it is from the original server or a copy.

```
getfrom = window.location.href;
alert(getfrom);
```

Which language does the user use

For some purposes, it is important to know which language the user uses.
You can check that with the next snippet:

```
var language = window.navigator.userLanguage ||
window.navigator.language;

alert(language)
```

Notes

HTML

A clear method to display your data

Often, we need a quick check of our data when testing a program. Most of the time, we will display the values of your data in an alertbox or in the console. When checking large amounts of data, this will get messy. Using JSON.stringify will display your data in a well-organized manner.

```
var temperature = 20;
var doorsensor = "closed";
var lamp = "off";

alert(JSON.stringify({temperature, doorsensor,
lamp}));
document.write(JSON.stringify({temperature,
doorsensor, lamp}));
console.log(JSON.stringify({temperature,
doorrsensor, lamp}));
```

This code displays an alertbox on the webpage, and in the console, the information is shown as follows:

{"temperatuur":20,"doorsensor":"closed","lamp":"off"}

Activate a link at a certain time

Suppose we are building a webpage where customers can order some goods, but only at at a certain time. We can put a link on the page to the actual ordering page. We want that link only to become active at a pre-defined time. We can achieve that as follows:

HTML Part:

```
<a id="activelink" title="<<You are too early>>"
target="_blank">
  This link activates at 17.00 hour
</a>
```

Javascript part:

```
<script>
  var link = document.getElementById('activelink');
  var actualtime = new Date().getHours();

  if (actualtime === 17)
  {
    link.href =
"http://lucstechblog.blogspot.com/";
    link.innerHTML="Go to Luc's Blog";
    link.title="Order now !!!";
  }
</script>
```

The script starts by searching the activelink on the page. Then we set the current time in a variable and compare that with 17 (17.00 hour). If the time is 17.00 hour we activate the link, change the text on the page and change the mouse tip.

Add an element to the bottom of the page

Use the next snippet to add a div to the end of a webpage. It does not need to be a div but can be any element like <p> <a> or <button>.

```
var addeddiv = document.createElement('div');
addeddiv.innerHTML = '<p>I am a new element</p>';
document.body.appendChild(addeddiv);
```

Add an element to a list

The next snippet shows how to add an element to a list. The text is fetched from an input field, and the program makes sure it is not empty.

HTML part:

```
<a>What do you want to add :</a>
<input id ="newtext" type="text" value =
"Javascript tips">
<button id = "newinlist">Add</button>
<br><br>Here is the list<br>
<ul id="thelist">
<li>ESP 32 Simplified</li>
<li>Raspberry Pi Pico Simplified</li>
</ul>
```

Javascript part:

```
<script>
document.getElementById("newinlist").addEventListen
er('click', additem);

function additem()
{
   var newelement =
document.getElementById("newtext").value;
   if (newelement !="")
      {
         var newli = document.createElement('li');
         newli.textContent = newelement;

document.getElementById("thelist").append(newli);
         newelement.value = "";
      }
}
</script>
```

Add an element to a list 2

Here is another method to add an item to a list.

HTML Part:

```
<input id="newtext" type ="text" value =
"Javascript tips">
<button id="newinlist">Add to list</button>
<ul id="thelist">
    <li>ESP32 Simplified</li>
    <li>Raspberry Pi Pico Simplified</li>
</ul>
<div id = "test"></div>
```

Javascript part:

```
<script>
var el = document.getElementById("newinlist");
el.onclick = makelist;
function makelist()
{
    var itemtoadd =
document.getElementById('newtext').value;
    var list = document.getElementById('thelist');
    var addthis = "<li>"+ itemtoadd +"</li>";
        list.insertAdjacentHTML('beforeend',
addthis);
    itemtoadd.value = '';
  }
</script>
```

Add or remove an event listener to an element

Using addEventListener() and removeEventListener(), we can add or remove eventlisteners to an element. The next example shows how to add a click event to a <p> web element.

HTML part:

```
<p id="test">
Click this text
```

```
</p>
```

Javascript part:

```
document.getElementById("test").addEventListener('c
lick',testclick);

function testclick()
{
alert("clicked")
}
```

Using removeEventListener() we can remove the eventlistener.

Add or remove a class

Using <style> we can set an element's attributes like font-size, color, etc.
Using a script, we can add, remove, or toggle that style. The next example
shows a web-page with a black text that changes to a red and larger font
when you press the button.

HTML part:

```
<head>
<style>
    .red
    {
        font-size: 25px;
        color: red
    }
</style>
</head>
<body>
<p id="colortext">Change the style by altering the
class</p>
<button class="alter">Click here</button>
<p>Click the button to change the class</p>
```

Javascrip part:

```
<script>

document.querySelector(".alter").addEventListener("
click", changeclass);
function changeclass()
{
    var element =
document.getElementById("colortext");
    element.classList.add("red");
}
</script>
```

If you want to remove the class just use: element.classList.remove("red");
You can toggle the <style> on and off with toggle :
element.classList.toggle("red");

Add text to an element

Generally, we use innerHTML to put a text into a field on the webpage.
This replaces the text that is already there. We can also choose to add text to
that field. Here is an example that adds text to a <div>

HTML Part:

```
<div id="textfield">Javascript</div>
```

Javascript part:

```
<script>
document.getElementById("textfield").innerHTML += "
tips and tricks";
</script>
```

Allow just one click on a button

Sometimes you want to prevent the user from clicking a button multiple times. The next snippet shows how to achieve this.

HTML part:

```
<h1>Test whether the button was pressed</h1>
<button  class="knop" >Click to test</button>
```

Javascript part:

```
<script>
document.querySelector(".knop").addEventListener("c
lick", pressed, { once: true });
function pressed()
{
alert ("You pressed the button");
}
</script>
```

When the button is clicked, the alert will show. If you click the button a second time, nothing happens.
You can use this not just with buttons but with any element on a page that can be clicked.

Alter the onclick function

Javascript can alter the onclick event of a button. Here is an example of how to do that.

HTML part:

```
<button id="test" onclick="function1()">
Click me
</button>
```

Javascript part:

```
<script>
function function1()
{
alert("This is not going to fire")
}
var newfunction = document.getElementById('test');
newfunction.setAttribute('onclick',  'alert("This
is the new alert");');
</script>
```

newfunction.setAttribute() overrules the, in the button defined, function call.

Automatically invoke the current year

Using new Date().getFullYear() gives us the current year. We can use this to automatically invoke the current year in (for example) a copyright message. The next example shows how this is done at the bottom of a page using innerHTML.

HTML part:

```
<p>
    At the bottom of this page<br>
    comes the copyright notice.<br>
    <br>
    <div id="autoyear"></div>
</p>
```

Javascript part:

```
<script>
var text = "Copyright "
var text = text + new Date().getFullYear();
document.getElementById("autoyear").innerHTML=text;
</script>
```

Automatically jump to the previous page

By putting the next code into your script the web browser will automatically jump to the previous page after 5 seconds (determined by the value 5000).

```
<SCRIPT>
setTimeout("history.back();", 5000);
</script>
```

Be careful with this code as it will be executed each time the user lands on the page.

Blocking an input field

You can check with onchange() if the text in an input field has changed.
You can then block the input by setting the original value back and ignoring the input.
The next example shows how to do this. This example does accept the input when a user tries to change it for the second time.

HTML part:

```
<INPUT id="inp" type="text" value= "do not change"
onchange="testchange()">
```

Javascript part:

```
<script>
var tries = 1;
function testchange()
{
    if (tries == 1)
    {
    alert("DON'T DO THAT");
    document.getElementById("inp").value="do not
change";
    tries = tries + 1;
```

```
    }
    else
    {
        alert("You made it")
    }
}
</script>
```

Change a text's attributes

HTML code allows you to set text attributes. With Javascript, we can change these attributes when the text is already displayed on the page. The next example changes part of a text in subscript.

```
<script>
var text = "example";
document.write("The following text in subscript:
"+text.sub());
</script>
```

The same way we can change other attributes:

```
document.write(text.small())
document.write(text.strike());
document.write(text.italics());
document.write(text.fontsize(10));
document.write(text.fontcolor( "blue" ));
document.write(text.bold());
document.write(text.big());
```

Change an elements id

The next snippet shows how to change an elements ID.

```
<script>
```

```
var element =
document.getElementById("originalID");
element.id = "modifiedID";
<script>
```

Change an image into another

You can change an image on a webpage into another image by changing the source url. Here is an example.

HTML part:

```
<img id="butimg"
src="https://i.postimg.cc/KzfwQZKS/butred2.png"
alt="Buttonred" width="500" height="333">
```

The above html code places a red button on the webpage.

Javascript part:

```
<script>
var imag = document.getElementById('butimg');
imag.src =
"https://i.postimg.cc/d16KhRwY/butblack2.png"
</script>
```

The script searches the image by its ID and puts its attributes into the variable imag. imag.src = "url" then changes the url in the url of another image.

Change the attributes of a text

To change the appearance of a text on a page in, for example, bold you can use CSS, but Javascript can do it also for you.

HTML part

```
<p id="becomeslarge">
  This text should be large
</p>
<button onclick="makelarge()">Make it so</button>
```

Javascript part:

```
<script>
function makelarge()
   {
   becomeslarge.innerHTML = "<h1>" +
becomeslarge.innerHTML + "</h1>";
   }
</script>
```

Change the background color of a webpage

Actually, this is not Javascript, but I would not keep it from you.
Using onmouseover="document.bgColor=' it is possible to change the
background color of a webpage when moving the mouse over an element on
that page.

Html part:

```
<a
onmouseover="document.bgColor='springgreen'">Green<
/a>

<a onmouseover="document.bgColor='plum'">Purple</a>

<a
onmouseover="document.bgColor='PowderBlue'">Blue</a
>
```

Change the background color of a webpage 2

This is just HTML code, not Javascript. The following HTML code will present a drop-down menu from which you choose the background color for the page.

```
<FORM>
<B>Choose a background color:</B>
<SELECT name="backcolor"
onChange=(document.bgColor=backcolor.options[backco
lor.selectedIndex].value)>
<OPTION value="C0C0C0" >Cool Grey
<OPTION value="0D09A3" >Dark Blue
<OPTION value="808040" >Avocado
<OPTION value="800080" >Purple
<OPTION value="444444" >Gray
<OPTION value="FF0400" >Red
<OPTION value="EFE800" >Yellow
<OPTION value="05EF00" >Green
<OPTION value="0206FF" >Blue
<OPTION value="AE08EF" >Violet
<OPTION value="FF8C8A" >Mauve
<OPTION value="FF80FF" >Pink
<OPTION value="FFCCCC" >Peach
<OPTION value="FFCC99" >Orange
<OPTION value="808080" >Dark Grey
<OPTION value="D5CCBB" >Tan
<OPTION value="DDDDDD" >LightGray
<OPTION value="FBFF73" >Light Yellow
<OPTION value="7CFF7D" >LightGreen
<OPTION value="A6BEFF" >Light Blue
<OPTION value="FFFFFF" >White
</SELECT></FORM>
```

Change the colors to your own liking. To easily find the hex codes for your color use the tool on this page:

https://www.rapidtables.com/web/color/RGB_Color.html

Change the background color by clicking a button

Using document.body.style.backgroundColor = "blue"; the background of a webpage is changed to blue. To change the background color by clicking a button, use the next code.

HTML part:

```
<button onclick="backgnd()">Click for a color
change</button>
```

Javascript part:

```
<script>
function backgnd()
   {
   document.body.style.backgroundColor = "blue";
   }
</script>
```

Change the background color of an element

To make an element stand out, you can change its background color after, for example, pressing a button. You can do this with element.style.backgroundColor = "color". The next snippet shows how to change the background color of the text of a <div> after pushing a button.

HTML part:

```
<div id="testdiv">
This background color will be changed
</div>
<button id="colchange" onclick="change()">change
the color</button>
```

Javascript part:

```
<script>

function change()
{
document.getElementById("testdiv").style.background
Color = "#ff0000";
}

</script>
```

This can be used on any element, and of course you can change the color to your own liking.

Change the background color of an input field after it is filled in

If a user clicks outside of an input field, or presses TAB, the background color of that field can be changed, to indicate that the user has filled it in. Use onblur to see if the field was left. Use text.style.background, where text is the field's ID, to change the background color.

HTML part:

```
<p>Put your text below:</p>
<input type = "text" id = "text0" onblur =
"colorise()">
```

Javascript part:

```
<script>
function colorise()
   {
   text0.style.background = "lightblue";
   }
</script>
```

274

Change the backgroundcolor on a page every x seconds

You can change the background color of a webpage every x seconds with the command setTimeout. The next snippet shows how to change the background color every 3 seconds.

Javasxcript part:

```
setTimeout("document.bgColor = 'deeppink'", 3000)
setTimeout("document.bgColor = 'red'", 6000)
setTimeout("document.bgColor = 'blue'", 9000)
setTimeout("document.bgColor = 'white'", 12000)
```

Change the color of an element by hovering the mouse over it

This is not Javascript but may come in handy when designing a web-page. The next snippet shows how to change the color of an element when you hover the mouse over it.

HTML part:

```
<html>
<head>
<style>
p:hover
{
    color: #FF0000
}
h1:hover
{
    color: #FF0000
}
</style>
</head>
```

```
<body>
<h1>Hover the mouse over this text</h1>
<p>And here also</p>
</body>
</html>
```

Change the color of several elements simultaneously

To change the color (or another attribute) of several elements on a webpage at the same, time use the following method. Start by giving the elements the same class name. We can then select them with that name. The next example shows how to do that.

HTML part:

```
<h2 class="tochange">This heading will change its
color</h2>
<p class="tochange">This paragraph too</p>
<div class="tochange">
<p>Anything in this div changes too.</p>
</div>

<button onclick="changethecolor()">Click to
color</button>
```

Javascript part:

```
<script>
function changethecolor()
{
var elements;
var i;
elements = document.querySelectorAll(".tochange");
for (i = 0; i < elements.length; i++)
  {
    elements[i].style.color = "red";
  }
}
```

```
</script>
```

Short explanation.
First, we catch all elements with the class name "tochange" in the array elements. Next, we iterate over the array and change the color of the elements text. This method can be used for changing all kinds of attributes of elements.

Change the fontsize and color of an element

Sometimes you want to emphasize something on a webpage when a user clicks on that element. You can achieve that with the following method:

HTML part:

```
<h1 onclick="change()">Change the font size and
color by clicking here</h1>
<button class="Btn" onclick="change()">CLICK
HERE</button>
<h3>Click the button to change its fontsize and
color</h3>
```

Javascript part:

```
<script>
function change()
   {
    event.target.style.fontSize = "32px";
    event.target.style.color = "red";
   }
</script>
```

The HTML function onclick tests if an element is clicked, and then calls the Javascript function change().

In Javascripts function change() the event.target knows which item has been clicked and the style part alters that elements size and color.

Change the color of an element

To make an element stand out, you can change its color after, for example, pressing a button. You can do this with element.style.color = "color". The next snippet shows how to change the color of the text in a <div> after pushing a button.

HTML part:

```
<div id="testdiv">
Text of which the background color will be changed
</div>
<button id="colchange" onclick="change()">change
the color</button>
```

Javascript part:

```
<script>
function change()
   {
   document.getElementById("testdiv").style.color =
"#ff0000";
   }
</script>
```


Change the mouse pointer

With just one simple command, we can change the looks of the mousepointer.

```
document.body.style.cursor = "default";
```

This sets the mouse pointer back in its default state.

Here is a list of choices of mousepointers that are available:

```
.alias {cursor: alias;}
```

```css
.all-scroll {cursor: all-scroll;}
.auto {cursor: auto;}
.cell {cursor: cell;}
.col-resize {cursor: col-resize;}
.context-menu {cursor: context-menu;}
.copy {cursor: copy;}
.crosshair {cursor: crosshair;}
.default {cursor: default;}
.e-resize {cursor: e-resize;}
.ew-resize {cursor: ew-resize;}
.grab {cursor: grab;}
.grabbing {cursor: grabbing;}
.help {cursor: help;}
.move {cursor: move;}
.n-resize {cursor: n-resize;}
.ne-resize {cursor: ne-resize;}
.nesw-resize {cursor: nesw-resize;}
.ns-resize {cursor: ns-resize;}
.nw-resize {cursor: nw-resize;}
.nwse-resize {cursor: nwse-resize;}
.no-drop {cursor: no-drop;}
.none {cursor: none;}
.not-allowed {cursor: not-allowed;}
.pointer {cursor: pointer;}
.progress {cursor: progress;}
.row-resize {cursor: row-resize;}
.s-resize {cursor: s-resize;}
.se-resize {cursor: se-resize;}
.sw-resize {cursor: sw-resize;}
.text {cursor: text;}
.url {cursor: url(myBall.cur),auto;}
.w-resize {cursor: w-resize;}
.wait {cursor: wait;}
.zoom-in {cursor: zoom-in;}
.zoom-out {cursor: zoom-out;}
```

Change the size of an image

If you need to change the width and height of an image, you can do that with the following commands:

```
var image = document.getElementById('id');
xval=100
yval=100
image.width=xval;
image.height=yval;
```

Start with identifying the image by its ID. Then use width and height to change its size.

Change the space between words

You can change the spacing between words with element.style.wordSpacing = "numberpx" You need to change numberpx in the number you need, like for example 25px.

Here is the element we are going to change:

```
<div id="text">Hello this is a test</div>
```

This is the code to change the spacing of the chosen element.

```
document.getElementById("text").style.wordSpacing = "25px";
```

Change the text of a button

You can change the text of a button, when the button is clicked. This way, the user knows the action has finished. You can do this by changing the innerHTML attribute of the button.

```
<button id="button0" type="button"
onclick="changetext()">Click to change</button>
```

Javascript part:

```
<script>
function changetext()
   {
document.getElementById("button0").innerHTML="Chang
ed text";
   }
</script>
```

Change text on a webpage

Sometimes, there is a text on a webpage you want to alter. The next example, which can easily be adapted, changes text in a <div> when a button is clicked.

Start with adding a button and a div with some text in your HTML code:

```
<button onclick="change()">Click here for changing
text</button>
<div id="changediv">Hi this is text 1</div>
```

Now add some Javascript in the <script> section on your page:

```
function changediv()
{
  var x = document.getElementById("mijndiv");
  if (x.innerHTML === "Hi this is text 1") {
    x.innerHTML = "Something different";
  } else {
    x.innerHTML = "Hi this is text 1";
  }
}
```

Each time the button is pressed, the text will change from Hi this is text 1, to Something different. This also works with other elements on your page like <p> and <a>.

Change text in bold

If you need to change the appearance of a text in bold, you can do that as follows.

```
var teststring = new String("this is the changed
text");
document.write("This text is normal:
"+teststring.bold());
```

The following variations are available:

```
document.write(teststring.small())
document.write(teststring.strike());
document.write(teststring.italics());
document.write(teststring.fontsize(10));
document.write(teststring.fontcolor( "blue" ));
document.write(teststring.bold());
document.write(teststring.big());
```

Clearing part of a webpage

Using innerHTML we can get information out of an object on a webpage or put information into that object. We can also use that to clear part of a webpage. This is done by document.body.innerHTML = ""; which replaces the body of the webpage with an empty string. Depending on where you put this command, everything before it will be erased and everything following it will stay visible.
Here is an example that clarifies this.

```
<html>
<head></head>
<body>

<p>This text will be erased</p>

<script>
document.body.innerHTML = '';
</script>

<p>This text will be shown</p>

</body>
</html>
```

Click on a button and execute a function delayed

Generally, you want a function to execute immediately when, for example, clicking a button. Sometimes, however, you want to delay the function for a certain time. This is how it is done.

HTML part:

```
<p>Click the button and wait for 3 seconds.</p>
<button onclick="delayfunc()">Try me</button>
```

Javascript part:

```
<script>
function delayfunc()
{
setTimeout(function(){ alert("Delayed for 3
seconds"); }, 3000);
}
</script>
```

Create a list and add items

The next snippet will create a list and add items to it that you can type in the input field.

HTML part:

```
<button id = "test">
click me for adding
</button>
<input id="inp">
<p id="listhere">HERE COMES MY LIST</p>
```

Javascript part:

```
document.getElementById("test").onclick  =
function()
{
  var node = document.createElement("Li");
  var text = document.getElementById("inp").value;
  var textnode=document.createTextNode(text);
  node.appendChild(textnode);
document.getElementById("listhere").appendChild(nod
e);
}
```

Create a random color

If you need a random color for your page or text, this is how you can create it.

```
function makecolor()
{
  var letters = '0123456789ABCDEF';
  var hexcolor = '#';
  for (var i = 0; i < 6; i++)
    {
```

```
        hexcolor += letters[Math.floor(Math.random()
* 16)];
    }
  return hexcolor;
}

var newcolor = makecolor();
alert(newcolor)
```

Copy a text to multiple elements

If you need to change text at several places on the webpage, you can do that
by giving all text fields the same class. The next example takes an input
field and puts the information from that field in several elements with the
same class name.

HTML Part:

```
<h1>Copy the text to multiple fields</h1>
<input type="text" class="lang" placeholder="Prog.
language" />
<button class="but">Preferred language</button>
<p    class = "lang">......</p>
<div class = "lang">......</div>
<a    class = "lang">......</a>
```

Javascript part:

```
<script>
var butele = document.querySelector(".but");
var langele = document.querySelectorAll(".lang");
butele.addEventListener("click", () =>
  {
    for (var i=1; i<langele.length; i++)
      {
      langele[i].innerHTML = langele[0].value;
      }
  });
```

```
</script>
```

Copy a text to the clipboard

The next lines of code show how you can copy a part of the webpage to the clipboard. From there, you can paste it in any other program

HTML part:

```
<input type="text" value="Hello world" id="mytext">
<button onclick="copyit()">Copy this text</button>
```

Javascript part:

```
function copyit()
{
  var copiedtext =
document.getElementById('mytext')
  copiedtext.select();
  document.execCommand('copy')
  console.log('Copied Text')
}
```

Count how many times the user scrolls up or down

Here follows a tip that you will not use often but may come handy at one time.
The code below has a variable called timesscrolled that counts how many times a user has scrolled the mousewheel (up and down) on the page.

```
var timesscrolled = 0;
window.addEventListener("wheel", function (action)
{
  var again = action.deltaY;
```

```
  if (timesscrolled> 0) {
    timesscrolled++;
  } else {
    timesscrolled--;
  }
  console.log(timesscrolled);
});
```

Create a new DOM element and give it an ID

The next example shows how to create a new element on a page. First, we determine where the element should come. This is done by selecting the element that comes before the new element. Then we create the new element with element.appendChild(). The element gets its ID with element.setAttribute("id", "id-naam"); This example also puts a button on the screen. Pressing the button changes the text of the freshly made element. This serves as an example to show how to make a new element and select it to change it. Alter it for your own purposes.

HTML Part:

```
<div id="new">
<p id="p1">ESP32 Simplified</p>
<p id="p2">Raspberry Pi Pico Simplified</p>
<button onclick="changetext()">Click to
change</button>
</div>
```

Javascript part:

```
<script>
var tag = document.createElement("p");
tag.setAttribute("id", "test");
var text = document.createTextNode("Here comes the
new text");
tag.appendChild(text);
var element = document.getElementById("p2");
element.appendChild(tag);
```

```
function changetext()
 {
document.getElementById("test").innerHTML="Javascri
pt tips"
 }
</script>
```

Create a paragraph on your webpage

If you need to put some text or data on a webpage, you can create a paragraph on the page where the text is placed. Here is an example that creates a paragraph with the text "Hello World", which is placed on the webpage after the <div> with the id "the-parent"

HTML part:

```
<div id=the-parent></div>
```

Javascript part:
```
<script>
var paragraph = document.createElement('p');
paragraph.innerHTML = 'Hello world';

document.getElementById('the-
parent').appendChild(paragraph);
</script>
```

To insert the paragraph before the div element you can use the next lines.

```
var paragraph = document.createElement('p');
paragraph.innerHTML = 'Hello world';

el = document.getElementById('the-parent')
el.parentNode.insertBefore(paragraph, el);
```

288

Delete an element from the webpage

The next snippet shows how to delete an element from your webpage. In this example, the page contains a button with the id but1 and a div with the id div1. Both elements are removed from the page when you click them.

HTML part:

```
<button id="but1", onclick="deleteme(this)">click
me</button>
<br>
<div id="div1", onclick="deleteme(this)">try
me</div>
```

Javascript part:

```
<script>
function deleteme(element){
   element.parentNode.removeChild(element);
}
</script>
```

Disable a button

To disable a button, you can use the command button.disabled=true. The next example puts a button on the webpage that will be disabled after you click it.

HTML part:

```
<button id="test" onclick =
clickfunc()>clickme</button>
```

Javascript part:

```
function clickfunc()
{
```

```
alert("Button is now disabled")
document.getElementById("test").disabled = true;
}
```

This is not limited to <button> but also works with other HTML tags like <input>

Disable an eventlistener

An eventlistener can be attached to an element to invoke an action. The eventlistener starts an action when an event happens, like, for example, a button is pressed or the mouse moves over an element. It is possible to disable that eventlistener when, for example, a condition is met. Disabling the eventlistener is done with element.removeEventListener You need to specify exactly which event you want to disable, as multiple events can be attached to one element.
The next example shows an alarm button that displays a message each time it is pressed. Next to that there is another button that will disable the eventlistener for the alarm button.

HTML part:

```
<p>Click the alarm button for a message<br>
Click on remove to disable the alarm</p>
<button id="alarm">Alarm</button>
<button onclick="removeevent()"
id="btnid">Remove</button>
```

Javascript part:

```
<script>
document.getElementById("alarm").addEventListener("
click", showalarm);
function showalarm()
   {
    alert("ALARM")
   }
function removeevent()
```

```
    {
document.getElementById("alarm").removeEventListene
r("click",showalarm);
    }
</script>
```

Disable the CTRL key

The CTRL key is used (amongst other functions) to copy and paste information. If you want to disable the CTRL key use the following code.

```
document.addEventListener("keydown", function
(event) {
          if (event.ctrlKey)
            {
              event.preventDefault();
            }
        });
```

Disable double clicking a button

The next snippet shows how to disable double clicking a button. To achieve this, we disable the button immediately when it is clicked. We can do that with element.disabled = true
To activate the button again, use element.disabled = false
The next example disables the button for 2 seconds after it has been clicked.

HTML part:

```
<button>Try me</button>
```

Javascript part:

```
<script>
const trybut = document.querySelector('button');
```

```
trybut.disabled = false;

trybut.addEventListener('click', function()
{
  trybut.disabled = true;
  alert("you clicked");
  setTimeout(() =>
    {
      trybut.disabled = false;
    }, 2000);
});
</script>
```

Disabling the right mouse button (copy and paste)

The right mouse button is used to copy and paste text and data. There will be moments when you want to prevent these functions. Using the following HTML code prevents the use of the right mouse button.

```
<body oncontextmenu="return false">
    <div></div>
</body>
```

This method can be overruled but will prevent most users from utilising copy and paste.
This can also be used on other parts of a page like:

```
<p oncontextmenu="return false">This text can not
be right-clicked</p>
```

Disable selecting and copying text with CSS

If there are certain parts of a text or another object that you want to prevent from being selected and copied, that can be done with some CSS code. The next example shows how to do that.

```
<head>
<title>Title of the document</title>
<style>
.unselectable
    {
    -webkit-user-select: none;
    -moz-user-select: none;
    -ms-user-select: none;
    user-select: none;
    }
</style>
</head>
<body>
<p>This text can be selected and copied</p>
<div class="unselectable">This text can not be
copied</div>
</body>
</html>
```

Using <div class="unselectable"> calls the CSS code which makes the object (div) un-selectable. The CSS code has several user-select: none lines that makes sure this works for all browsers.

Disable selecting and copying text with Javascript

You can disable selecting and copying text with CSS, and you can can do it with pure HTML as the next example shows. The commands we use for that is onmousedown="return false" and onselectstart="return false"

```
<!DOCTYPE html>
<html>
<head>
</head>
<body>
<p>This text can be selected and copied</p>
<div onmousedown="return false"
onselectstart="return false">This text can not be
selected and copied</div>
```

```
</body>
</html>
```

Put this command in the body section of the webpage, and selecting and copying are prevented for the whole page.

```
<!DOCTYPE html>
<html>
<head>
</head>
<body onmousedown="return false"
onselectstart="return false">
<p>This text can not be selected and copied</p>
<div>This text can not be selected and copied</div>
</body>
</html>
```

Display a scrolling text

The next program shows how to continually scroll text from left to right across the screen. The text, size, color, and speed, can easily be adjusted.

HTML part:

```
<body onload="scroll()">
<h1 style="color:red; font-size:50px;">
<pre id="scrolltext">Javascript Tips        </pre>
</h1>
```

Javascript part:

```
<script>
function scroll()
{
   text =
document.getElementById("scrolltext").innerHTML;
setInterval(function ()
    {
```

```
        text = text[text.length - 1] +
text.substring(0, text.length - 1);

document.getElementById("scrolltext").innerHTML=tex
t;
    }, 200);
}
</script>
```

Display text gradually faster

To emphasize a portion of a page, we can have a text appear letter by letter and increase the speed at every letter. Here is an example that achieves this.

HTML part:

```
<h1>Faster and faster</h1>
<button class="textbutton">Click to start</button>
<h2 class="textlocation"></h2>
```

Javascript part:

```
<script>
document.querySelector('.textbutton').addEventListe
ner('click',typeText);
    var i = 0;
    var text = "This text will appear faster and
faster to emphasize that something is happening
here";
    var length = text.length
    var speed = 50+ length *5;
    function typeText()
{
        if (i < text.length)
        {

document.querySelector('.textlocation').innerHTML
+= text.charAt(i);
```

```
                i++;
                setTimeout(typeText, speed);
                speed=speed-5;
        }
}
</script>
```

A short explanation of the most important parts. Using var length = text.length determines the length of the text. The program then multiplies this value by 5 and adds 50. This determines the initial speed. Alter this to your own likings. next document.querySelector('.textlocation').innerHTML += text.charAt(i); puts the letters one by one on the screen. Every time a letter appears speed=speed-5; decreases the speed. The speed is then used with setTimeout(typeText, speed); to slow down the function.

You can alter this by starting at an initial speed of 0 and slowing down with speed=speed=5; Again, adjust to your own liking

document.getElementById("elements ID") is not strictly necessary.

To select an element from a webpage, we start by giving the element an ID. In our code we use that ID to search the element with document.getElementById("ID of element") and then do something with it. But that is not perse necessary. You can use the ID itself to select the element.

HTML Part:

```
<button id="testbut" type="button"
onclick="changeit()">Click to change</button>
```

Javascript part:

```
<script>
function changeit()
    {
        testbut.innerHTML="New text";
```

```
      testbut.style.background = "skyblue";
  }
</script>
```

This example shows how the text and color of a button change when you click it. We do not use document.getElementById("ID of element") but use the ID of the button.

Enable or disable buttons or input fields

Sometimes you want to enable a button, radiobutton or inputfield etc. after a certain action has completed. The document.getElementById('ID').disabled = true; command disables the element. And with document.getElementById('ID').disabled = false; you can enable the element. The next example puts 3 buttons on a webpage. The On and Off buttons activate or de-activate the Try Me button.

HTML part:

```
<p>
<input id="but01" type="button" value="Try Me"
onClick="buttonclick();"></input>
</p>
<input  id="but02" type="button" value="ON"
onClick="butenable();"></input>
<input  id="but03" type="button" value="OFF"
onClick="butdisable();"></input>
```

Javascript part:

```
<script>
function butdisable()
   {
    document.getElementById('but01').disabled =
true;
   }
function butenable()
   {
```

```
      document.getElementById('but01').disabled =
false;
  }

function buttonclick()
  {
    alert ("The button works")
  }
</script>
```

Fill a table with an array

If you need to fill a table on your HTML page with the contents of an array, you can use the following method.
In this example, the array consists of multiple objects that have the name of the month (month), the temperature (tmp), and rain information (rain).

```
var testarray = [
  { month:"Jan", tmp:"10", rain:"yes" },
  { month:"Feb", tmp:"15", rain:"yes" },
  { month:"Mar", tmp:"20", rain:"no" },
];
```

Here is the complete HTML page that achieves this.

```
<!DOCTYPE html>
<html>
<head>
</head>

<body>

    <table style="width:25%" id="table1">
    <tbody></tbody>
    <thead>
        <th>Month</th>
        <th>Temperature</th>
        <th>Rain</th>
```

```
        </thead>
        </table>

</body>
<script>

var testarray = [
    { month:"Jan", tmp:"10", rain:"yes" },
    { month:"Feb", tmp:"15", rain:"yes" },
    { month:"Mar", tmp:"20", rain:"no" },
];

var tabfil = "";
for (i=0; i<testarray.length; i++)
{
    tabfil = tabfil +
"<tr><td>"+testarray[i].month+"</td><td>"+testarray
[i].tmp+"</td><td>"+testarray[i].rain+"</td></tr>";
}
document.querySelector("#table1 tbody").innerHTML =
tabfil;

</script>
</html>
```

It looks more complicated than it is.
Start by defining the table in the HTML body part.

The script iterates over every array element.
The variable tabfil is first filled with <tr> which starts a new row in the
table. Next <td> is added which starts a new column, and each column is
filled with the contents of the object.

Flatten an array

If you need to flatten a multi dimensional array, you can do that with
array.flat(). Here is an example that shows how this works.

```
var array = [1, 2, [3, 4, [5, 6, [7, 8, [9,
10]]]]];
array = array.flat()
alert (array)
```

Force focus to an input field

Sometimes, you need to force the user to pay attention to a certain input field. For example when the field is left empty or filled in with a wrong value.

The next example shows 3 input fields and pressing the button forces the focus to field 2:

HTML part:

```
Give your Name:<input type="text" id="input1"
value="Luc"><br>
Give your Addres:<input type="text" id="input2"
value="Somestreet"><br>
Give your Place:<input type="text" id="input3"
value="Earth"><br>
<br>
<button type="button" onclick="check()">Select Text
Box</button>
```

Javascript part:

```
<script>
function check()
   {
     document.getElementById("input2").select();
   }
</script>
```

Format HTML code in a string with multiple lines

To format HTML code neatly we split it over multiple lines. If you want to put the code into a variable that will pose some problems.

```
var htmlcode = "<p>
   A random text.
</p>";
```

The lines above will give an error in Javascript. To solve that put a backslash at the end of each line like the following snippet demonstrates.

```
var htmlcode = "<div>\
   A random text.\
</div>";
```

Get the selected text

If you need to get the part of a webpage (text) that has been selected, highlighted with the mouse, by the user, you can use the next command:

```
text = window.getSelection().toString();
```

Here is an example that gets the text when the user highlights a text and then presses a key

```
document.onkeypress = function ()
{
text = window.getSelection().toString();
alert(text)
}
```

Get a value from a table

To get a certain value out of a cell in a table you can use document.getElementById("tablename").rows[X].cells[Y]. The table must have an ID, and the row and column must be known. The following example shows how you can get the information:

HTML part:

```
<table style="border:4px solid red" id="testtable">
        <tr>
            <td>Red</td>
            <td>Blue</td>
        </tr>
        <tr>
            <td>Green</td>
            <td>Yellow</td>
        </tr>
</table>
<p>
<input type="button" onclick="getcellvalue()"
value="Show the color">
</p>
```

Javascript part:

```
<script>
function getcellvalue()
   {
     var cellvalue =
document.getElementById("testtable").rows[1].cells[
1];
     alert(cellvalue.innerHTML);
   }
</script>
```

Get mouse coordinates in the page or in an element

Using clientX and clientY we can get the mouse coordinates. The next program shows how to get the coordinates to call a function when the mouse moves (onmousemove). The function places the coordinates in an <h2> tag.

HTML part:

```
<body onmousemove = "getcoord(event)">
<h2 id="textfield"></h2>
<p>Above are the X and Y coordinates of the mouse
location</p>

<br><br><br><br><br><br><br><br><br><br><br><br>
```

Javascript part:

```
<script>
function getcoord(event)
   {
     var x_pos = event.x;
     var y_pos = event.y;
     var xypos = "X position= " + x_pos + ", Y
position = " + y_pos;

document.getElementById("textfield").innerHTML =
xypos;
   }
</script>
```

By putting onmousemove = "getcoord(event)" in the <p> tag, for example, the coordinates will only change (on the screen) when you move the mouse over the text of the <p> tag.
The
 's in the page are only there to give the page some body.

Get the screen resolution

If you need to know the screen resolution, you can use the next commands that put the resolution in the variables width and height.

```
var width = window.screen.availWidth;
var height = window.screen.availHeight;
```

Get the dimensions of an img before it is loaded

The next snippet shows how to get the dimensions of an image before you put it on the webpage.

```
function getdimensions(url, callback)
{
    var img = new Image();
    img.src = url;
    img.onload = function() { callback(this.width,
this.height); }
}

getdimensions
(
  "https://i.postimg.cc/KzfwQZKS/butred2.png",
  function(width, height)
  { alert(width + 'px ' + height + 'px') }
);
```

Get the window resolution

You might want to know what the resolution is of the window you are working in. The next snippet shows how to get that information.

```
x = window.innerWidth
```

```
y = window.innerHeight

alert("Width : " + x + " Height : " + y);
```

ID is only valid for 1 element

If you give several elements on a page the same ID, only the first element will be associated with that ID.

HTML part:

```
<h1 id="id01">Only here works the ID</h1>

<p id="id01">This text has the same ID but does not
react on it/p>

<button id="id01">Just try it</button>
```

Javascript part:

```
<script>
document.getElementById("id01").addEventListener("c
lick", function() {
   alert("Here ID01 works");
});
</script>
```

Only clicking the first line will activate the function.
If you need multiple elements to react use class like described in previous tips.

Hide an element when clicking on the webpage

To hide an element on a page when clicking on that page, you can use element.style.display = 'none' You need to exchange element for the name of the part you want to hide. You can use this to hide any element you want like <div>, <a>, <p>, <h1> or any other element. The next example shows how to hide a div.

HTML part:

```
<div id="vanish">Click on the page and the text
disappears.</div>
```

Javascript part:

```
<script>
window.onload = function()
  {
    var divvanish =
document.getElementById('vanish');
    document.onclick = function(e)
      {
        if(e.target.id !== 'vanish')
          {
            vanish.style.display = 'none';
          }
      };
  };
</script>
```

Hide an element by clicking a button

The next example shows how to hide an element from the webpage when clicking a button. The element is chosen by its ID

HTML part:

```
<h2>Let an element disappear</h2>
<p id="demo">This will disappear.</p>
<button type="button" onclick="gone()">Click Me!
</button>
```

Javascript part:

```
<script>
function gone()
{
document.getElementById('demo').style.display='none
';
}
</script>
```

Hide multiple elements on a page

We can hide an element on a webpage with element.style.display = 'none'.
By giving multiple elements the same class name, we can hide several
elements at the same time.

HTML part:

```
<div class= "remove">Element 1</div>
<div class= "remove">Element 2</div>
<br>
<button onclick="hideclass()">Hide
elements</button>
```

Javascript part:

```
<script>
function hideclass()
  {
    var removeclasses =
document.querySelectorAll('.remove');
```

```
    var i = 0;
    var l = removeclasses.length;

    for (i; i < l; i++)
      {
      removeclasses[i].style.display = 'none';
      }
  }
</script>
```

To show all the elements again use removeclasses[i].style.display = 'block';

How many elements in a dropdown menu

Using document.getElementById("dropdown").length; we can get the number of elements in the dropdown menu with the ID "dropdown".

HTML part:

```
<select id="dropdown">
  <option>C++</option>
  <option>Javascript</option>
  <option>Python</option>
</select>
```

Javascript part:

```
<script>
var number =
document.getElementById("dropdown").length;
document.write("Elements in dropdown list: "+
number);
</script>
```

How many images on this page

Using document.images.length you can determine how many images are present on a page. You can use that as follows.

HTML part:

```
<img
src="https://cdn.pixabay.com/photo/2021/08/13/12/51
/sea-6543041_960_720.jpg">
<img
src="https://cdn.pixabay.com/photo/2021/07/23/17/07
/volcano-6487743_960_720.jpg">
<img
src="https://cdn.pixabay.com/photo/2021/08/12/10/38
/mountains-6540497_960_720.jpg">
<img src="https://javascript-
tips.weebly.com/uploads/3/2/1/8/3218777/published/b
alkjs.jpg?1624135861">
```

Javascript part:

```
<script>
var number = document.images.length;
document.write("<br>Number of images on this page:
"+number);
</script>
```

How many rows in a table

We can check that with tablename.rows.length how many rows there are in a table. The next program shows how to get that number.

HTML part:

```
<table id="testtable" border="5">
<thead>
```

```
<tr>
<th>Month</th>
<th>Temp</th>
</tr>
</thead>
<tbody>
<tr><td>Jan</td><td>17</td></tr>
<tr><td>Feb</td><td>16</td></tr>
<tr><td>Mar</td><td>18</td></tr>
<tr><td>Apr</td><td>20</td></tr>
</tbody>
</table>
```

Javascript part:

```
<script>
var datatable =
document.getElementById("testtable");
var numberrows = datatable.rows.length;
alert("The number of rows = "+numberrows);
</script>
```

Be aware that the table header is also counted as a row. So in this case the alert will show 5, rows while there are actually 4 rows with data.

How much time does the user spends on the webpage

If you want to measure how much time a user is spending on your webpage, you can use the following example.

HTML part:

```
<p id="timeonsite"></p>
```

Javascript part:

```
<script>
var now;
```

```
var time;
var difference;
var seconds;
var minutes
window.onload = showit;
now = new Date().getTime();
function showit()
  {
    time = new Date().getTime();
    difference = ( (time - now) / 1000) | 0;
    minutes = ( (difference / 60) | 0);
    difference = difference %60;
    seconds ="" + ( (difference > 9) ? difference :
"0" + difference);
document.getElementById("timeonsite").innerHTML =
minutes + ":" + seconds;
    setTimeout("showit()",1000);
  }
</script>
```

innerHTML not always shows all information

Using innerHTML we can retrieve text from a page. That can also be done
with innerText and textContent. But be aware that you will not always get
the information you are looking for. Take a look at the following example:

HTML part:

```
<p id="test">This text contains a tag <CENTER>some
test text</CENTER></p>
```

Javascript part:

```
<script>
alert(document.getElementById("test").innerHTML);
alert(document.getElementById("test").innerText);
alert(document.getElementById("test").textContent)
</script>
```

All three alerts show: "This text contains a tag" and the rest of the text is lost.

However if the tag is an <a>, <b>, <i> or <span> you will get the right information.

Input does not use innerHTML

Well, the heading of this tip shows what it is. If you need to get information out of an input field you can not use innerHTML. Use value instead.

```
document.getElementById("test").value
```

Input field with increase and decrease

Input fields are made for getting information from a user. Here is an input field with arrows that increase and decrease the value. The example takes that value and performs a calculation on it.

HTML part:

```
<h1>Celsius to Fahrenheit</h1>
<h2>Enter the temperature in Celsius</h2>
Temperature

<input
id="enter"
type="number"
size="5"
placeholder="0"
oninput="celtofar(this.value)"
onchange="celtofar(this.value)"/>

<br>
<br>
```

In Fahrenheit is that: <span
class="fahrenheit"></span>

Javascript part:

```
<script>
function celtofar(valuecelsius)
   {

document.querySelector(".fahrenheit").innerHTML =
((valuecelsius * 1.8)+32).toFixed(2);
   }
</script>
```

Insert a new element before or after an existing element

It is easy to put a new element on a webpage. We can indicate where we want to put the new element by putting it in front of an element with a known ID. The next snippet shows how to put a new <p> element before another <p> element with the ID "last"

HTML part:

```
<p>The first element</p>
<p id="last">The last element</p>
```

Javascript part:

```
<script>
function inbetween(where, what)
   {
   where.insertAdjacentHTML('beforebegin', what);
   }
var where = (document.getElementById("last"));
var what = "<p> A new element </p>";
inbetween(where,what);
</script>
```

By replacing

```
where.insertAdjacentHTML('beforebegin', what);
```

with

```
where.insertAdjacentHTML('afterend', what);
```

the new element is placed behind the <p> element.

Insert a text before an existing element

Here is an example of how you can insert a line of text (or another element) before an element for which the ID is known

This is the webpage:

```
<h1>
Headline of the page
</h1>
<div id="test">
This is a line of text
</div>
```

The next code inserts the text "This comes first" before the div on the page.

```
var element = document.getElementById('test');

var inserttext = document.createElement('p');
    inserttext.innerHTML = 'This comes first';

element.parentNode.insertBefore(inserttext,
element);
```

Insert a row in a table

It may happen that you need to add a row with data to an existing table. The next example has a table with the following values:
One   Two
Three Four
Seven Eight

Suppose we want to add the values Five and Six at the right location. Using var variable = document.getElementById(x).insertRow(2); we declare a variable that inserts the second row in the table.

```
var leftcel = newrow.insertCell(0);
var rightcel = newrow.insertCell(1);
leftcel.innerHTML = "Five";
rightcel.innerHTML = "Six";
```

These lines define the new cells and put the right values in them. The next example shows how the row with cells is inserted after pressing a button.

HTML part:

```
<table style="border:4px solid red" id="testtable">
        <tr>
            <td>One</td>
            <td>Two</td>
        </tr>
        <tr>
            <td>Three</td>
            <td>Four</td>
        </tr>
        <tr>
            <td>Seven</td>
            <td>Eight</td>
        </tr>
</table>

<p>
```

```
<input type="button"
onclick="addnewrow('testtable')" value="Add another
row">
</p>
```

Javascript part:

```
<script>
function addnewrow(x)
   {
   var newrow =
document.getElementById(x).insertRow(2);
   var leftcel = newrow.insertCell(0);
   var rightcel = newrow.insertCell(1);
   leftcel.innerHTML = "Five";
   rightcel.innerHTML = "Six";
   }
</script>
```

Make an element appear and disappear

The command style.display = "none" makes an element on your webpage
disappear. To have it re-appear you can use style.display = "block"
The next example makes text in a <div> disappear when you push the
button.

HTML part:

```
<div id="top">This is a test </div>

<button onclick="toggle()">Click and text
disappears</button>
```

Javascrip part:

```
<script>
function toggle()
   {
```

```
   document.getElementById("top").style.display =
"none";
   }
```

```
</script>
```

Make an element appear and disappear 2

The previous tip demonstrated how to have elements on a page appear and disappear. The disadvantage was that the element was removed from the page, and all remaining information on the page scrolled upwards. To avoid this, you can use element.style.visibility = "hidden"; This does not remove the element from the page but only makes it invisible.
element.style.visibility = "visible"; makes the element visible again in the same location where it was so the rest of the page does not alter position. The next snippet shows how to use this.

HTML part:

```
<p id = "examtext">Example text</p>

<button type = "button" onclick =
"textgone()">Hide</button>
<button type = "button" onclick =
"textshow()">Show</button>
```

Javascript part:

```
<script>
function textgone()
   {
document.getElementById("examtext").style.visibilit
y = "hidden";
   }

function textshow()
   {
```

```
document.getElementById("examtext").style.visibilit
y = "visible";
    }

</script>
```

Move the caption of a table

The caption of a table is generally at the top. Using
element.style.captionSide = "bottom" we can change its position to the
bottom.

```
<html>
    <body>
        <table id = "languages" >
            <caption id = "title">2021
Courses</caption>
            <tr>
                <th>Programming languages</th>
            </tr>

            <tr>
                <td>C++</td>
            </tr>

            <tr>
                <td>Javascript</td>
            </tr>

            <tr>
                <td>Python</td>
            </tr>
        </table>
        <br>

        <button onclick = "changepos()">Click to move
the caption</button>
```

```
<script>
    function changepos() {

document.getElementById("title").style.captionSide
= "bottom";
    }
</script>

</body>
</html>
```

Move the mouse over an element to jump to another webpage

This is not Javascript but nevertheless something that might become useful.

Use this code to jump to another webpage, in this case my weblog, when you hover the mouse over an element.

```
<div target=main onmouseover="window.open
 ('http://lucstechblog.blogspot.com/');"
>http://lucstechblog.blogspot.com/</div>
```

This will work with all elements on a webpage like <p>, <a>, <h1> etc.

Move the mouse over an element to trigger a function

Using onmouseover, you can test whether the mouse is located on an element on the page. Using onmouseout tests if the mouse is no longer on that element. The next example shows how to use these commands to trigger a function to change the color of an element on the page and change it back.

HTML part:

```
<p onmouseover="over()" onmouseout="out()">Move the
mouse over this text to change it's color.</p>

<div onmouseover="over()" onmouseout="out()">
<h2>Try this text to</h2>
</div>
```

Javascript part:

```
<script>
function over()
  {
    event.target.style.color = "red";
  }
function out()
  {
    event.target.style.color = "black";
  }
</script>
```

Open a new webpage

Using window.location.href = "URL" we can force Javascript to open
another webpage. The next example shows how to do that after pressing a
button.

HTML part:

```
<h1>Open a different webpage</h1>
<button onclick="doit()">Go to my page</button>
```

Javascript part:

```
<script>
function doit()
  {
```

```
    window.location.href
="http://lucstechblog.blogspot.com/";
 }
</script>
```

Open a new webpage 2

If you need to open another webpage in a new tab, you can use the following command:

```
window.open('http://lucstechblog.blogspot.com/',
'_blank');
```

Perform a different function each time an element is clicked

.onclick = executes a function when a button or element gets clicked. We can change .onclick = to execute each time a different function.

HTML part:

```
<button id="clickme">Click Me</button>
```

Javascript part:

```
<script>
function one()
  {
    alert('one clicked');
    document.getElementById('clickme').onclick =
two;
  }

  function two()
  {
```

```
   alert('two clicked');
   document.getElementById('clickme').onclick =
one;
   }


   document.getElementById('clickme').onclick = one;
</script>
```

In the button definition no function is called. That is done in the script by document.getElementById('clickme').onclick = one; When clicked function one is executed and in there the function call is changed in function two. When the button is clicked again function two is activated, and that changes the call back to function one. This makes the button click alternately call function one and function two.

Prevent space from scrolling

Normally, when you press the space bar somewhere in a webpage, the browser will scroll one page down. That is the default function of the space bar. If you want to prevent this from happening you can use preventDefault() like this:

```
window.addEventListener('keydown', function(e)
{
   if(e.keyCode == 32 && e.target == document.body)
   {
     e.preventDefault();
   }
});
```

Password protected page

The next example shows how you can build a very simple protection for your webpages. A prompt asks for a password and compares that with a predefined password. If it matches the if() command will redirect the page to another webpage. If the match is false, in this example, you will be directed to yet another webpage. This is a very simple protection that anybody with a bit of knowledge of Javascript can break. You only have to open the page source with your browser and look at the code. However, it will stop most of the users.

HTML part:

```
<body>
MY page
```

Javascript part:

```
<script>
var password;
var pass1 = "luc";

password=prompt("Type your password:","");
if (password==pass1)
   {
     window.location=
"http://lucstechblog.blogspot.com/";
   }
else
   {
   window.location= "https://javascript-
tips.weebly.com/";
   }
</script>
```

Print the current page

The drop down menu of your webbrowser has a print function. However, sometimes you want to make things more convenient for the end-user by putting a print-button on the web-page. This can be done easily with inline Javascript:

```
<input type="button" value="Print This Page"
onClick="window.print()" />
```

Put the above line in the body of your HTML code.
You can also put a button on the webpage, and make it call a function that
prints the page when pressed. This can be done as follows:

HTML part:

```
<button onclick="sayHello()">Click me</button>
```

Javascript part:

```
<script>
function sayHello()
{
    window.print();
}
</script>
```

Put a comma separated text as a list on screen

The next program shows how we can put a list on a webpage that is made
from a text with comma separated words.

```
<!DOCTYPE html>
<html>
<body>
<div id="listspace"> </div>
<script>
    var text = "C++ , Javascript, Lua, Python"
    var textarray = text.trim().split(',')
    var newlist = '<ul>'
    for (var i=0; i<textarray.length; i++)
    {
        newlist += '<li>' + textarray[i] + '</li>';
    }
    newlist += '</ul>';
```

```
    document.getElementById("listspace").innerHTML =
newlist;
</script>
</body>
</html>
```

Put an element at a window's X-Y coordinate.

Using the CSS style you can place an element at an X and Y coordinate on a window. First determine the element by selecting it by its ID and then place it at the desired position with style.left and style.top. The next snippet shows how to use this.

```
<!DOCTYPE html>
<html>
<div id="divtest">This is a test</div>
<script>
    var element =
document.getElementById('divtest');
    element.style.position = "absolute";
    element.style.left = 100 + 'px';
    element.style.top = 100 +'px';
</script>
</body>
</html>
```

The element is in this example placed at the co-ordinates style.left 100 which is the X value, and style.top 100 which is the Y value. Make sure to add "px" to the figure as the position is determined in pixels.

Refresh the page

You can refresh the current web-page with the next command:

```
window.location.reload();
```

Remove an option from a drop-down menu

A drop down menu offers the user several options. Using the next example, you can remove options after a choice has been made.

HTML part:

```
<select id = "menu" onChange = "remove()">
   <option>Make your choice</option>
   <option>C++</option>
   <option>Javascript</option>
   <option>Python</option>
</select>

<p>Make a choice and it will be removed</p>
```

Javascript part:

```
<script>
function remove()
   {
     var x = document.getElementById("menu");
     x.remove(x.selectedIndex);
   }
</script>
```

Remove an element from the webpage

Maybe after a text has been read, or a function has been executed, you want to remove that specific text, or any other element, from the webpage. Using document.querySelector("#element") you can select the element, and with elem.remove(); you can remove that element. The next example puts text and a button on a webpage, and when the button is clicked, both are removed.

```
<!DOCTYPE html>
<html>
<body>
```

```
<p id="test">This text is going to be removed</p>
<button id="test2" onclick="removetext()">Click
me</button>

<script>
  function removetext()
  {
  var elem = document.querySelector("#test");
  elem.remove();
  var elem = document.querySelector("#test2");
  elem.remove();
  }
  </script>
    </body>
</html>
```

Remove an element from the webpage 2

The previous tip showed how to remove an item from a webpage by
selecting it with document.querySelector(). The same can be done with
document.getElementById() as the next sample shows.

```
<html>
<body>
<p id="p1">Python</p>
<p id="p2">Javascript</p>
<script>
    var first = document.getElementById("p1");
    var second = document.getElementById("p2");
    first.remove();
</script>
</body>
</html>
```

Two elements (with id's p1 and p2) are placed on the page and then the first
element is removed.

Remove all elements with a certain class

Using document.querySelectorAll() we can select all elements with a certain class. They are put in an array and can then all be removed from the webpage.

HTML part:

```
<p class="test">This text is going to be
removed</p>
<button class="test" onclick="vanish()">Click
me</button>
```

Javascript part:

```
<script>
  function vanish()
  {
    var elem, i;
    elem = document.querySelectorAll(".test");
    for (i=0; i < elem.length; i++)
    {
      elem[i].remove();
    }
  }
</script>
```

As the text and the button have the same class, they both will be removed.

Remove elements between two elements

This example has a webpage with several elements. Some elements have been given an ID. If you need to remove elements that are situated between elements with a known ID you can use the next example.

HTML part:

```
<div id="1">START</div>
```

328

```
<p>Language 1: Basic</p>
<p>Language 2: C++</p>
<p>Language 3: Javascript</p>
<p>Language 4: Lua</p>
<p>Language 5: Python</p>
<div id=2>END</div>
```

Javascript part:

```
<script>
var startingPoint = document.getElementById("1");
var endingPoint = document.getElementById("2");
while (startingPoint.nextElementSibling &&
startingPoint.nextElementSibling !== endingPoint)
{
    startingPoint.nextElementSibling.remove();
}
</script>
```

All the elements between

```
<div id="1">START</div>
```

and

```
<div id=2>END</div>
```

are removed from the page.

Repeatedly react on addEventListener()

To repeatedly react on addEventListener() the best option is to call each time a function.

HTML part:

```
<p id="texthere">0</p>
<button id="button1">Click to increase</button>
```

Javascrip part:

```
<script>
var counter = 0
function testfunc()
 {
    counter = counter +1;
document.getElementById("texthere").innerHTML=count
er;
 }
var butpress = document.querySelector("#button1");
   butpress.addEventListener("click", testfunc);
</script>
```

Each time the addEventListener() is activated it calls the function testfunc().

Replace an image with another

If you want to replace an image with another image, you can do that, as demonstrated in the following example.

HTML part:

```
<img id="image1"
src="https://images.pexels.com/photos/1116440/pexel
s-photo-1116440.jpeg?
auto=compress&cs=tinysrgb&dpr=1&w=500" width="400"
height="200">
<button onclick="replacepic()">Replace
image</button>
```

Javascript part:

```
<script>
function replacepic()
   {
    var imgReplace =
document.getElementById("image1");
```

```
   imgReplace.width = 400;
   imgReplace.height = 150;
   imgReplace.src =
"https://images.pexels.com/photos/3889990/pexels-
photo-3889990.jpeg?
auto=compress&cs=tinysrgb&dpr=1&w=500";
   }
</script>
```

Replace an image with another 2

In Javascript there is often more than one way to achieve something. This tip shows an alternate method for replacing an image with a different one. The previous tip assumed we know the ID of the picture. If we do not know that we can get the number of pictures on a page with the following command:

```
var numpic = document.images.length;
```

To alter the third picture and its size we can use the following commands:

```
document.images[2].width = 100; // new width
document.images[2].height = 100; // new height
document.images[2].src= "link to a picture";
```

To iterate over the images ID's for finding a particular one you can use the following loop:

```
<script>
function replacepic()
{
    var numpics = document.images.length;
    for (var i=0; i<numpics;i++)
    {
        alert(document.images[i].id);
    }
}
</script>
```

Rotate an object on a webpage to draw attention

To draw attention to an object, you can rotate the element when the page is loaded, or when a button is clicked, etc. The next script shows how to rotate a text when the page is loaded.

HTML part:

```
<h1 id="turn" style= "color:red";>Round and round
goes the text</h1>
<h2>The text above will turn the amount of degrees
which you can set in the script</h2>
```

Javascript part:

```
<script>
var turntext = document.getElementById("turn");
var turndegrees = 360;
var anglenow =100;

setInterval(function()
{

if (anglenow < turndegrees)
  {
    anglenow += 1;
    turntext.style.transform =
'rotate('+anglenow+'deg)';
  }
}, 1);
</script>
```

The text in the <h1> tag starts at 100 degrees (anglenow) and turns to 360 degrees (turndegrees). It starts tilted. Set the value of anglenow to 0, and it will start horizontal and turn all the way round. The setInterval() function ends with the figure 1, which determines the speed of rotation. A higher figure brings a slower rotation.

Rotate the complete webpage

It is possible to rotate the complete webpage upside down. This is the command that achieves that:

```
document.getElementsByTagName('body')
[0].style.transform = 'rotate(180deg)';
```

You can replace 180deg by any angle you want. The word "deg" must be included for this to work.

To paraphrase Google: OK Javascript do a barrel roll !!!!

Run a function when the window closes

The next function runs just before the window closes. You can use that for example to save variables before the user closes the window.

```
window.onbeforeunload = closefunc;
function closefunc()
{
    // do what you need to do
    return null;
}
```

Run multiple functions with one button click

Usually, you will call a function when a button is clicked. But what if you want to run two functions when you click the button? You can achieve this to call a function that then calls two other functions. Here is how to achieve that.

HTML part:

```
<button onclick="twofunctions()">Click me</button>
```

Javascript part:

```
<script>
function twofunctions()
  {
    action();
    another();
  }
function action()
  {
    alert("Function action 1")
  }
function another()
  {
    alert("Another one")
  }
</script>
```

Set or clear a radiobutton

Normally, a user can check or clear a radiobutton by clicking it. This can however, also be done with Javascript. In this example, the radiobutton is selected by it's ID

```
document.getElementById("ID").checked = false;
document.getElementById("ID").checked = true;
```

Set or erase the hin in an input field

The next code shows how a hint is set into the input field when the user clicks next to it. When the user clicks into the field, the hint is erased.

HTML part:

```
<p>Programming language:</p>
<input id="proglang" value="What language ">
```

Javasctipt part:

```
<script>
function gotfocus()
 {
   if (this.value == this.defaultValue)
   this.value = '';
 }
function nofocus(event)
 {
    if (this.value == '')
    this.value = this.defaultValue;
 }
var event = document.getElementById('proglang');
event.onfocus = gotfocus;
event.onblur = nofocus;
</script>
```

Set the maximum length of an input field

If you need to restrict the length of the input from a user's text, you can set the length of the input field.

```
<input id="test">
Type something
</input>

document.getElementById('test').setAttribute('maxle
ngth', 10);
```

Select any text on your screen and use it

The next example shows how you can select any text on your screen, push a button and use that text for other purposes. Selecting text can be done with: window.getSelection().toString()

HTML part:

```
<button id="newinlist" onclick = "gettext()">Select
any text and click</button>
<ul>
  <li>ESP32 Simplified</li>
  <li>Raspberry Pi Pico Simplified</li>
</ul>

<div>This is a longer text with some trivial
sentences in it</div>
```

Javascript part:

```
<script>
function gettext()
  {
    var selectedtext =
window.getSelection().toString();
    alert(selectedtext);
  }
</script>
```

Scroll to the top of a page

Sometimes a web-page offers, at the bottom, of the page a button that brings you direct to the top of the page. This can easily be done with window.scrollTo(0,0) The figures (0,0) are the start coordinates of any webpage. The next example shows an almost empty web-page with a button at the bottom. Press the button, and a function is called that uses the window.scrollTo(0,0) command to immediately bring you back to the top of the page.

HTML part:

```
<p>Click the button to scroll to the top</p>
<br><br><br><br><br><br><br><br><br><br><br><br><br
><br><br><br><br><br><br><br><br><br><br><br><b
r><br><br><br><br><br><br><br><br><br><br><br><
br><br><br><br><br><br><br><br><br><br><br><br>
<br><br><br><br><br><br><br><br><br><br><br><br
><br><br><br><br><br><br><br><br>
<button onclick="totop()">To the
top</button><br><br>
```

Javascript part:

```
<script>
function totop()
{
   window.scrollTo(0, 0);
}
</script>
```

Scroll to the bottom of a page

The following command lets you jump to the bottom of the webpage:

```
window.scrollTo(0,document.body.scrollHeight);
```

Show a message if the drop-down menu selection has changed

With onchange, we can test whether a user has altered a choice in a drop-down menu. We can use this to show a message, but this can easily be altered to call a function.

```html
<html>
<head>
</head>
<body>
<select onchange="alert('You changed your mind');">
  <option>choose your favorite language</option>
  <option>C++</option>
  <option>Javascript</option>
  <option>Python</option>
</select>
<p>Choose an option to test.</p>
</body>
</html>
```

Show one or multiple messages when a webpage is opened

There are occasions when you want to show an alert after the HTML page is opened. You can use this for a notification or to remind the user that he has to do something. For certainty, you can show a message a bit later after the page has been opened.

Using the setTimeout() function, you can show an alert after a certain time. Put the following lines into your script and wait for the alerts:

```javascript
setTimeout(function(){alert("test")}, 8000)
setTimeout(function(){alert("test number two")}, 3000)
```

Despite the fact that the order is different "test number two" will be shown first (after 3 seconds), and 5 seconds later, the second alert will appear.

Show or hide an element

Maybe you want to show or hide an element on a webpage, depending on the situation. Using style.display = "block" shows an element on the page, while style.display = "none" makes it disappear. The following example demonstrates how to let a <div> element appear or disappear on pressing a button.

HTML part:

```
<p>Press the button to show or hide an element</p>
<button onclick="goneandback()">Click me</button>
<br><br>
<div id="hideshow">
The magic element
</div>
```

Javascript part:

```
<script>
function goneandback()
{
  var elemstate =
document.getElementById("hideshow");
  if (elemstate.style.display === "none")
  {
    elemstate.style.display = "block";
  }
  else
  {
    elemstate.style.display = "none";
  }
}
</script>
```

Show or hide the contents of an input field

You do not want to display the input of a user on your screen if the information he needs to enter is secret, like a password. In that case, we can mask the contents of the input field with bullets like the next snippet shows.

HTML part:

```
<h1 style ="color: red">Show or not</h1>
Password:
<input type="password" value="secret" id="entrance"
/><br /><br />
<input class="check" type="checkbox" />Show it
<h2>Click the checkbox to show or hide</h2>
```

Javascript part:

```
<script>

document.querySelector(".check").addEventListener("
click", shownow);
function shownow()
  {
    var infield =
document.getElementById("entrance");
    if (infield.type === "password")
      {
        infield.type = "text";
      }
    else
      {
          infield.type = "password";
      }
  }
</script>
```

As you can see, the only thing you have to do is check with if (entrance.type === "password") whether the type of the inputfield = "password" if that is so, it is set to masking bullets. With entrance.type = "text"; the contents of the input field is changed to normal text again.

Show when a page was last changed

A lesser-known HTML command is document.lastModified. This command shows when a webpage is modified. We can show this information on a webpage, which can be valuable for the users.

```
<script>
document.write( "<B>Last modification "+
document.lastModified +"</B>");
</script>
```

The <B> makes the text appear in bold letters.

Simulate a click on an element

The next snippet shows how to simulate a click on an object in software.

```
document.getElementById("myelement").click();
```

Please note that this does not work on <a> tagged elements.

Start a function immediately when a page is loaded

Sometimes, you want to start a function as soon as the webpage is loaded. The next code shows how that can be done.

```
<!DOCTYPE html>
<html>
<title>Run function when page loads</title>
<head>
    <script>
        function runimmediate() {
            alert('ok');
        }
        window.onload = runimmediate;
```

```
        </script>
    </head>
    <body>
    </body>
    </html>
```

Start a function when the whole page has loaded

Sometimes, you want to wait before starting a function untill the whole page is loaded. The next snippet shows how to do that:

```
document.addEventListener("DOMContentLoaded",
function()
{
  alert("The document has been loaded");
});
```

Start multiple functions with one mouse-click

It is possible to start multiple functions at the same time with one mouse click. To do so, separate the functions with a ; The next example shows how it is done

```
<html>
    <head>
        <script>
            function function01()
            {
                document.write ("First function.
<br>");
            }
            function function02()
            {
                document.write ("Second function");
            }
```

```
    </script>
  </head>
  <body>
      <p>Click the button to see the result</p>

        <input type = "button" onclick =
"function01(); function02()" value = "Click to
start">

    </body>
</html>
```

Test if a button was clicked

There are several ways to test if a button was clicked. The onclick function is one way. Using document.querySelector(".button").addEventListener("click", functionname); is another valid way. In the next example, we test for a class name.

HTML part:

```
<h1>Check if button was clicked</h1>
<button class="BUTTON">Test the button</button>
```

Javascript part:

```
<script>
document.querySelector(".BUTTON").addEventListener(
"click", buttonpressed);
function buttonpressed()
{
alert ("Yes the button was clicked");
}
</script>
```

Test if the checkbox is checked

A checkbox is ideal for making a fast choice. The next snippet shows how to test if the checkbox has been checked or not.

HTML part:

```
<h1>Test a checkbox</h1>
Confirm: <input type="checkbox" class="choice"
onclick="testchoice()" />
```

Javascript part:

```
<script>
function testchoice()
  {
    if (document.querySelector(".choice").checked ==
true)
      {
        alert("confirmed");
      }
    else
      {
        alert("not chosen");
      }
  }
</script>
```

The line if (document.querySelector(".classname").checked == true) tests whether the checkbox has been checked or not, and shows an alert depending on the state.

Test if a key was pressed

If you need to test if a key was pressed, regardless which key it was, use this snippet.

```
document.addEventListener("keypress", function()
{
      alert("pressed")
});
```

Test if a key was pressed 2

If you need to test if a key was pressed anywhere on the webpage, use the next snippet.

```
document.onkeypress = function (e)
{
  alert("pressed")
};
```

Test if a key was pressed and which key that was

Using document.onkeypress we can check if anywhere on the webpage a key was pressed. The next snippet shows which key that was.

```
document.onkeypress = function (eventKeyName) {
   eventKeyName = eventKeyName || window.event;
   if(eventKeyName.keyCode==13){
       alert('You pressed the ENTER key');
   } else {

alert(String.fromCharCode(eventKeyName.keyCode))
   }
};
```

Test if the Alt, Control or Shiftkey were pressed

The next snippet shows how to test if the Alt, Control, or Shift keys are pressed when you click on a text on the screen.

HTML part:

```
<p onmousedown="testspecial(event)" >
Keep Alt, Control or Shift pressed and<br>
click this text</p>
```

Javascript part:

```
<script>
   function testspecial(event)
   {
      if (event.altKey)
      {
         alert("ALT pressed");
      }
      if (event.shiftKey)
      {
         alert("Shift pressed");
      }
      if (event.ctrlKey)
      {
         alert("Control pressed");
      }
   }
</script>
```

Test if the Backspace key was pressed

The next snippet shows an alarm when the BACKSPACE is pressed.

```
document.addEventListener("keydown", function
(event) {
```

```
        if (event.key == "Backspace") {
            console.log("Backspace Pressed");
        }
})
```

Test if the Enter key was pressed in an input field

If you want to know if the user pressed enter in an input field, you can use the next example.

HTML part:

```
<input id="test"> test</input>
```

Javascript part:

```
<script>
var inputelement = document.getElementById("test");
inputelement.addEventListener("keyup",
function(event)
{
    if (event.key === "Enter")
       {
           alert("You pressed enter")
       }
});
</script>
```

Test for an empty input field

The user can enter information using an input field. We must verify that the input field is not empty before we can use that data. The following example demonstrates how to test that.

HTML part:

```
Input Name <input id="input1" type="text">
<br>
Input Nickname <input id="input2" type="text">
<br>
<button onclick="testinput()" >Fill in and
click</button>
```

Javascript part:

```
<script>
function testinput()
  {
    if(document.getElementById("input1").value ==
"")
      {
        alert('Fill in your name please.');
        document.getElementById("input1").focus();
      }
    else
      {
      if(document.getElementById("input2").value ==
"")
        {
         alert('Fill in the nickname please');
         document.getElementById("input2").focus();
        }
      }
}
</script>
```

The button's click causes the testinput() function to run. If
(document.getElementById("input1").value == "") is used in this function
to determine whether the input field is empty. If that is so, a warning is
shown. The input field then gets the focus. The page will scroll to that point,
no matter where on the page the input field is.

Test if the wondow has changed size

If you want to know if a user has changed the window size, you can listen for the window.resize event.

```
window.addEventListener('resize', function(event){
    var newWidth = window.innerWidth;
    var newHeight = window.innerHeight;
    alert(newWidth);
    alert(newHeight);
});
```

Test if Javascript is activated

There are sometimes reasons to deactivate Javascript. And there are some TOR browsers that deactivate Javascript automatically. A lot of functionality will not work if JavaScript is disabled. We can test if Javascript is activated and give the user a warning if it is not.

```
<script>
    document.write("Javascript is activated, you
have full functionality")
</script>

<noscript><h1>JavaScript is disabled. Please turn
it on for full functionality</h1></noscript>
```

Put these lines in the <head> or <body> part of your HTML code and the user will get a welcome message dependent of Javascript functionality.

Three methods to generate a click event

There are 3 methods to generate a click event on an element on a webpage.

Method 1:

```
<div id="element">Click me</div>

<script>
document.getElementById('element').onclick =
function()
{
    alert('click');
}
</script>
```

Method 2:

```
<div id="element">Click me</div>

<script>
var el = document.getElementById("element");
el.addEventListener('click', function()
{
  alert("click");
});
</script>
```

Method 3:

```
<div id="element">Click me</div>

<script>
var el = document.getElementById("element");

el.onclick = function()
{
  alert("click");
}
</script>
```

It does not matter which version you use. For clarity, be consistent and always use the same code in a program.

Trigger a button click

By using the right code, we can let our program trigger the button click. You can do that with: document.getElementById("buttonid").click(); The next snippet shows how to do that.

HTML part:

```
<p onmouseover="pressed()">Move the mouse over this
text to simulate pressing the button</p>
<button type="button" id="testbutton"
onclick="pressed()">Click me to test</button>
```

Javascript part

```
<script>

function klikknop()
{
    document.getElementById("testbutton").click();
}

function pressed()
{
  alert("The button has been pressed.");
}

</script>
```

Pressing the button activates an alert with the text: The button has been pressed. Moving the mouse over the text simulates clicking the button. Be careful in using this function !!

Which key was pressed

To help a user navigate or make choices, we can ask them to press a key. We need to find out which key was pressed. The next program shows how to do that:

351

HTML part:

```html
<h1>Which key was pressed</h1>
<p id="demo"></p>
<div>
Press a key to see its Keycode
</div>
```

Javascript part:

```javascript
<script>
var texthere = document.querySelector("#demo");
document.body.addEventListener("keydown", whichkey)

    function whichkey(event)
    {
    switch (event.keyCode)
      {
          case 37:
             texthere.innerHTML = "Left arrow";
          break;
          case 38:
             texthere.innerHTML = "Up arrow";
          break;
          case 39:
             texthere.innerHTML = "Right arrow";
          break;
          case 40:
             texthere.innerHTML = "Down arrow";
          break;
          case 8:
             texthere.innerHTML = "Backspace";
          break;
          case 13:
             texthere.innerHTML = "Enter";
          break;
          default:
             texthere.innerHTML = "Keycode = " +
event.keyCode;
      }
    }
```

```
</script>
```

The last line in the switch test (texthere.innerHTML = "Keycode = " +
event.keyCode;) shows the Keycode so you can easily adapt this to your
own scripts.

A helpful website for finding keycodes is: **https://keycode.info/**

What choice was made in a drop-down menu

The next example shows how to determine which choice a user made in a
drop-down menu. The alerts show the index of the menu.

```html
<html>
<body>
<select id="choose">
  <option>C++</option>
  <option>Javascript</option>
  <option>Python</option>
</select>

<input type="button" onclick="display()"
value="Make your choice">

<p>Click the button to show the chosen index</p>

<script>
function display()
 {
    var index =
document.getElementById("choose").selectedIndex;
    alert(index);
            }
</script>
  </body>
</html>
```

Change :

```
var index =
document.getElementById("choose").selectedIndex;
```

into :
```
var index =
document.getElementById("choose").value;
```

and the alert shows the name of the choice we made.

Wait a certain amount of time

Unlike other languages, Javascript has no sleep or delay functions. Nevertheless, you can activate a function after a certain time. The method to use for this is

setTimeout(function() {}, (x * 1000));

The variable x determines the amount of seconds before the function runs.

```
var number1 = 10;
var number2 = 20;
var sum = number1 + number2;

setTimeout(function() {alert("the sum of the
addition = " + sum );
}, (10 * 1000));
```

In the above example, the calculation is done immediately, but the result is shown after 10 seconds. Please bear in mind that the main program runs on, and therefore the values of number1 and number2 might have altered in between.

Which key was pressed

A previous tip showed how to display the keycode of a pressed key. Keycodes are numbers. But what if you want to get the actual letter or function of that key. Just replace the script part by:

```
<script>
var texthere = document.querySelector("#demo");
document.body.addEventListener("keydown", whichkey)

    function whichkey(event)
    {
            texthere.innerHTML = event.key;
    }
</script>
```

event.key returns as a string the key that was pressed. You will get the letters a-z, the figures 1-0, and all punctuation marks. Next to that event.key also returns the names of special keys like: Shift, Enter, Control, Alt, Delete, Insert, ArrowUp etc.

Which page is this

Sometimes a website or a webpage gets copied. And you might want to know if the current Javascript code runs from the original page or from a copy. This is how you can check the URL:

```
var currentUrl = window.location.href;
```

Notes about HTML

Liability

This book and the tips, snippets, and programs in it are composed with the most possible care. Nevertheless, it may occur that information in this book is outdated or contains other inaccuracy's. Building and using the programs, snippets, and examples in this book are your own responsibility. The author, printer, publisher and bookseller can not be held liable for any damage (direct or indirect) that arises from using the information in this book.